MARI
SSB
OPERATION

G000155074

A Small Boat Guide to
OCEAN YACHT
Communications

J. Michael Gale

fernhurst
B O O K S

Copyright © Fernhurst Books 2004

First edition published in 1992,
with a second edition published in 1997

by

Fernhurst Books,	Phone: 44 (0) 1903 882277
Duke's Path, High Street,	Fax 44 (0) 1903 88 2715
Arundel, West Sussex,	e-mail: sales@fernhurstbooks.co.uk
BN18 9AJ, UK	website: www.fernhurstbooks.co.uk

British Library Cataloguing in Publication Data:
A catalogue record for this book is available from the British Library

ISBN 1–904475–03–5

Printed & bound in China through **World Print**
The moral right of J. Michael Gale to be identified as the author of this work has been asserted
in accordance with ss 77 and 78 of the Copyright, Designs and Patent Act 1988

The Publisher is pleased to acknowledge and thank the following people and organisations for
their help in the preparatation of this book, others are thanked in the Acknowledgements:
Barrett Communications Pty Ltd, J. Michael Gale, ICOM-UK Ltd, ICS Electronics Ltd, INMARSAT
Ltd, McMurdo Ltd, Simrad Ltd

Jacket Design by Simon Balley
Designed, Edited & Typeset by John Carden
Set in 9/11 pt Rockwell

**Sailing is an activity that has inherent risks and dangers. While this publication intends to
provide information on how to sail and use sailing equipment safely, the Publishers and
Distributors can not and do not guarantee that the inherent risks and dangers will be
completely limited by following the information in this book. The Publishers and Distributors
do not assume any responsibility or liability to the reader for any sailing accident. The reader
should understand that the information in this book is of a general nature and that it is the
responsibility of the reader to use his or her own good judgement in safely applying this
general information to the individual facts of any given sailing situation presented**

The ITU naterial on p. 77 has been reproduced with the prior authorization of the International
Telecommunications Union as copyright holder. The sole responsibility for selecting extracts for
reproduction lies with the beneficiary of this authorization alone and can in no way be
attributed to the ITU. The complete volume of the ITU material from which the map reproduced
is extracted, can be obtained from: International Telecommunications Union, Sales & Marketing
Division, Place des Nations, CH–1211, Geneva 20, Switzerland. Tel: +41 22 730 61 41, Telex: 421
000 uit ch, Fax +41 22 730 51 94, e-mail: sales @itu.int, website:http://www.itu.int/publications

Contents

Preface to the

3rd edition

For the past 100 years, sea rescues were hurriedly 'cobbled together' on a local, ad hoc basis much like the rescue of the *Titanic*. Maritime countries 'did their own thing' – if they did anything at all!

Finally, the International Maritime Organization (IMO) introduced the Global Maritime Distress and Safety System (GMDSS) in 1992 with full mandatory implementation for ships over 300 gross tonnage on 1 February 1999. So now at last, safety of life at sea is properly organized and co-ordinated on a world-wide basis.

The message is to 'join' the GMDSS as soon as possible if you value your own life and that of your friends and family. Having trained hundreds of professional and leisure sailors in the GMDSS, I can assure you that it is not an ogre to be feared. Only the initial calling procedure has been changed - considerably eased and improved by the use of digital technology. Traditional voice communications procedure has not changed. So, 'old hands' need only spend a little time learning new calling techniques. Read on to see how this new technology integrates with traditional R/T procedures.

J. Michael Gale, G3JMG,
BoT Yachtmaster (Ocean)
Hayling Island,
July, 2003

ACKNOWLEDGEMENTS

Firstly, I must thank my Wife, Jean, for her patience, tolerance and understanding during the many long hours she spent alone, often on sunny days, whilst I sat upstairs typing (with one finger) in my back bedroom 'shack'.

(Radio rooms are always called 'shacks' since the early days of marine radio when the 'radio room' was a wooden shed on deck!)

For much help and advice in the preparation and checking of the notes of the first edition, grateful thanks must also go to the following:

Alan Clemmetsen of ICS Electronics, Ltd.

Chris Sutton and Peter Crafter of CAS (UK), Ltd.

Larry Bennett of Portishead Radio

Ian Marshall of Locat Developments, Ltd.

Paul Frost of Icom (UK), Ltd.

Bill Hall, G4FRN, UK Maritime Mobile Net

Mike Dennison. G3XDV, Radio Society of Great Britain

Geoff Hales, editor and yachtsman of renown

Tim Davison, Publisher and hundreds of students for badgering me into writing this book

Many thanks also to Kim Fisher, UK Maritime and Coastguard Agency, for his valuable help in the preparation of the GMDSS Chapter in the Second and Third Editions.

For help in the preparation of this Third Edition thanks also to Andrew Marshall of the Warsash Nautical Bookshop, UK.

1

Why SSB?

Why buy an SSB (Single Sideband) set as well as a VHF (Very High Frequency) radio? The answer, quite simply, is increased range. Most readers will be aware that VHF radio waves travel in straight lines like light waves. Consequently, their range on Earth is determined almost entirely by the height of the respective aerials (antennae): the higher the aerials, the further the 'line of sight' will clear the Earth's curvature. Figure 1.1 shows this relationship which is discussed further in Chapter 6.

For greater ranges beyond the horizon, lower frequencies must be used. So, in addition to VHF, Marine Radio also uses the Medium Frequency (MF) or Medium Wave (MW) Band and the High Frequency (HF) or Short Wave (SW) Band. We will see in Chapter 3 that High Frequency implies short wavelength and vice versa.

Medium Waves tend to follow the curvature of the Earth; the range being determined by the power transmitted (Figure 1.2). The Marine MF Band gives a range of about 0.75 mile per watt and, as the maximum power allowed in the MF Band at sea is 400 watts, this means a maximum range of about 300 miles.

Like VHF, Short Waves also travel in straight lines but, additionaly, are 'bounced'

Figure 1.1 VHF 'line-of-sight range; the higher the aerial, the greater the range

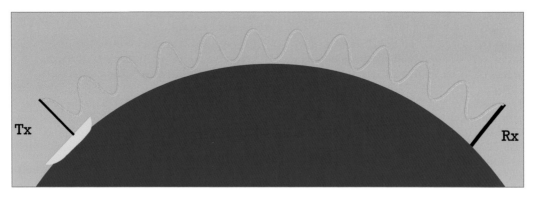

Figure 1.2 MF ground wave mode: the range is proportional to power

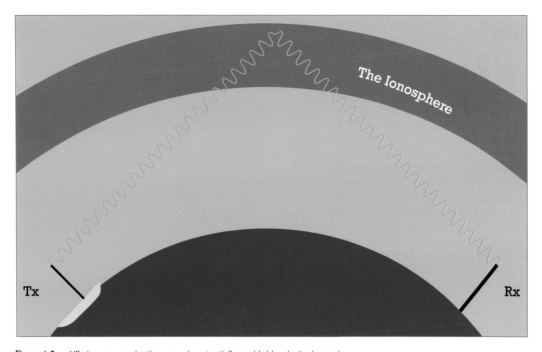

Figure 1.3 HF sky wave mode: the range is potentially worldwide, via the ionosphere

off the Ionosphere high above the Earth's surface to return to Earth several hundred or several thousand miles away (see Figure 1.3 and Chapter 4).

Consequently, Medium Waves give medium range and Short Waves give long range. In practical terms, a good guide is as follows:

❑ Up to 30 miles, VHF is preferred (clear speech, ease of use).
❑ For 30 – 300 miles range, MF (MW) is most suitable.
❑ For ranges over 300 miles, HF (SW) must be used.

Marine SSB sets operate on MF and HF. Marine VHF sets are physically separate (i.e. are in different boxes!) as they use frequency modulation.

SAFETY

Since the late 1890s, ad hoc distress and safety services operated firstly on 500kHz in Morse code, by voice on 2182kHz from the 1920s then Channel 16 VHF from the 1950s. The minimum mandatory range for MF was only 150 miles: HF was voluntary! In 1999, the Global Maritime Distress and Safety System (GMDSS) became mandatory for all passenger vessels on international voyages and for cargo vessels over 300 tons. This now gives worldwide safety coverage using voice or text on MF, HF, VHF and satellites. Although not mandatory for small craft, prudent owners should join the GMDSS 'club'. Details in Chapter 7.

AMATEUR RADIO

Only the holder of an Amateur Radio licence can legally chat freely and directly from a boat to someone at a great distance (ashore or afloat) who must also be a licensed Radio Amateur. It is necessary to pass a written technical exam to obtain this licence. The international requirement for a Morse code test was rescinded on 4 July 2003. Most of the popular oceanic sailing areas (North Atlantic, Pacific, Mediterranean, etc.) are covered by unofficial (but highly effective) Maritime Mobile 'Nets'. These are networks of shore-based Amateur Radio Stations who control frequent and regular chat sessions with their counterparts afloat known as 'Maritime Mobiles'. In addition to exchanging news about the weather, other yachts, good/bad places to berth/eat/drink, etc., these 'Nets' have also been instrumental in effecting some rescues. Amateur Radio is, therefore, an extremely useful and enjoyable supplement (but not an alternative) to professional Marine Radio for those with an aptitude for electronics. Be warned, though. Like many other skilled hobbies such as golf, snooker, computer games, etc., Amateur Radio can easily become addictive. Not so much a hobby, more a way of life! See Chapter 12.

OTHER SERVICES

In addition to being able to talk to other ships, harbours, marinas, yacht clubs and make telephone calls to the shore via the international network of Coast Radio Stations, possession of a Marine SSB Radiotelephone opens up a whole new world of other services and facilities such as TELEX/Fax/E-mail, NAVTEX, Weatherfax, time signals, etc. which are covered in Chapter 11.

2

What is SSB?

Single sideband radiotelephones are much more complex to operate than VHF sets and, unlike motor vehicles, their controls are not standardized. With some, frequencies are selected by rotary knobs while others use push buttons. With simplex-only transceivers (combined transmitter-receivers), the transmit and receive frequencies, which are often different, are selected simultaneously (as with VHF) whereas with duplex equipment, the transmitter and receiver may have to be controlled separately. This is good in the respect that it allows technical progress but makes it difficult to train operators. An operator could be trained on one type, like a monkey, but would be completely lost when faced with another. So, some basic technical knowledge is necessary for competent operation.

Audio Frequencies (AF)

Vocal chords create air-pressure waves to which our ears respond. To understand the mechanism, consider a single musical note. A note played on, say, a flute or a piccolo creates waves of air pressure which are heard as a single tone. When analysed, these waves are seen to be a succession of alternate compressions and rarefractions. This is easily seen by picking up the sound with a microphone which converts the air pressure waves into electrical pressure waves of alternating current (AC) and displaying them on an oscilloscope. What is seen is a succession of gentle undulations called sine waves. The excursion in pressure from the mean level at any point to the maximum pressure, through the mean to the minimum pressure and back to the mean again (working from left to right) constitutes one cycle of operation (Figure 2.1). How often this occurs (the *frequency*) is measured in cycles per second (c/s) or *Hertz* (Hz) in honour of Dr Heinrich Hertz, an early German pioneer (1Hz = 1c/s).

The human ear responds to audio frequencies between 20Hz and about 20,000Hz (or 20 kiloHertz – 20kHz) with the pitch of the note increasing with frequency. Above that, the human ear loses interest although other animals such as dogs and bats can hear higher frequencies. Human hearing becomes impaired with age and can be damaged by working in a noisy environment, the effect being to reduce the upper-frequency limit. No problems are experienced, however, unless the upper-frequency response falls to below 3kHz which is the upper limit of human speech. This effect is experienced by the hard of hearing who can hear low frequency vowels, which convey little information, but cannot hear the high frequency consonants which convey most information. To sufferers from this complaint it sounds as though their correspondent is talking through a cushion!

Just as a flute's audible tone can be converted into an electrical sine wave by means of a microphone, the reverse process

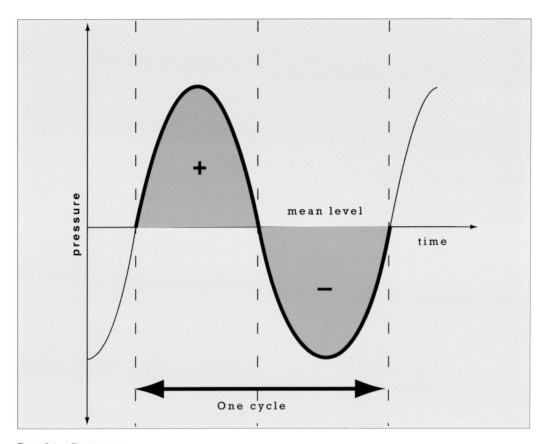

Figure 2.1   The sine wave

is also possible. An audio frequency sine wave can be generated by an electronic circuit and converted into sound waves by means of a suitable transducer such as a loudspeaker or telephone earpiece.

Radiotelephony (R/T) starts with the human voice which comprises a range, group or *band* of *audio frequencies* (AF). As this is the *basic band* of communication frequencies, it is called the *baseband* (Figure 2.2a).

RADIO FREQUENCIES

When alternating current is passed along an electrical conductor, some of the energy is converted into *electro-magnetic radiation* which radiates into space rather like the heat lost from the pipes supplying hot water to a central heating system. At the very low power supply frequencies of 50Hz or 60Hz, this loss of energy through radiation is negligible but radiation increases with increasing frequency.

Although this radiation of energy is bad for electrical engineering, it is just what radio engineering is all about! For radio use, however, this radiation does not begin to become efficient until the upper limit of audibility is reached. For example, the lowest radio frequency in general service is the Omega navigation system on, roughly, 10kHz. For most purposes, however, much higher frequencies are used.

Problem: *The high radio frequencies (RF) will travel through space but cannot be heard whereas the much lower audio frequencies (AF) can be heard but will not travel!*

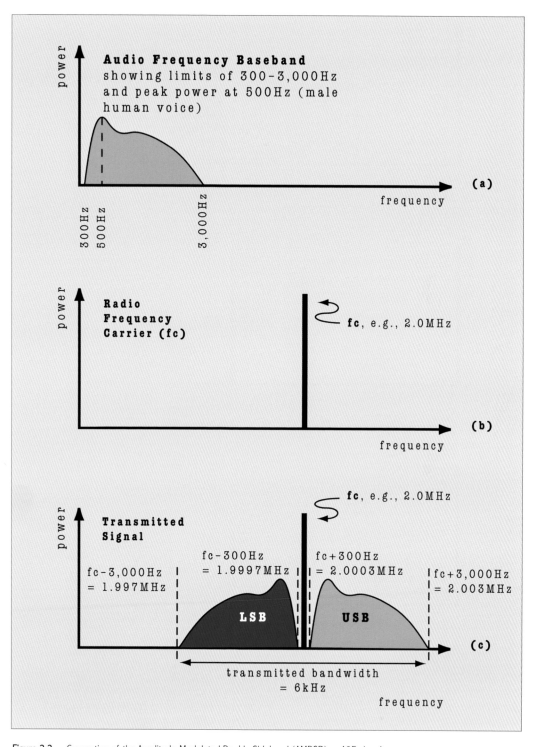

Figure 2.2   Generation of the Amplitude-Modulated Double Sideband (AMDSB) or A3E signal

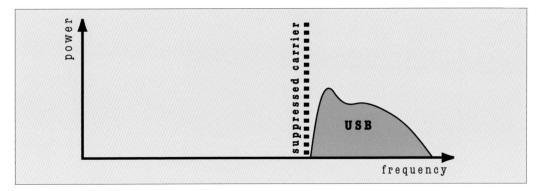

Figure 2.3   Single sideband suppressed carrier (SSB) or J3E signal

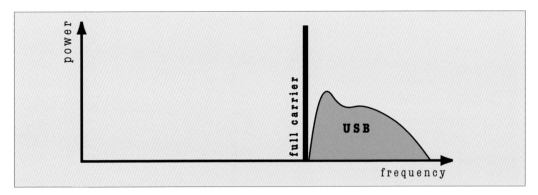

Figure 2.4 Compatible SSB or H3E signal

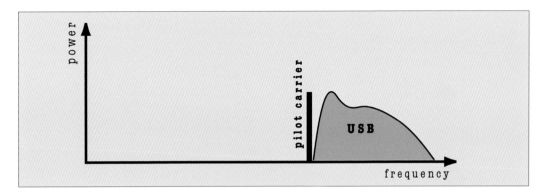

Figure 2.5   Pilot-carrier SSB or R3E

MODULATION

The solution is to *add* the small band of audio frequencies – 300-3,000Hz in the case of human speech – to a radio frequency *carrier* which is generated within the transmitter

(Figure 2.2b). Thus the speech (or music) 'rides on the back' of the carrier just like a messenger on horseback. This process is called *modulation* and there are several techniques commonly used. Historically the oldest system, called *amplitude modulation*

(AM) is still used for long wave, medium wave and short wave broadcasting as it is, by present standards, low-tech and cheap. Until the 1970s, AM was also used for marine communication but not now.

Double Sideband (A3E)

When a band of audio frequencies is added to a radio frequency carrier, two *sidebands* are created; one on either side of the carrier. The *upper sideband* (USB) slightly higher in frequency than the carrierr, is the sum of the carrier and audio or *baseband* and the *lower sideband* (LSB) the difference between the carrier and baseband frequencies. (This just happens; nature decreed it thus.) The resultant is commonly called AM. Its full title is *amplitude modulated double sideband* (AMDSB) or A3E signal. Like most low-tech systems it is simple, effective, reliable and cheap but it is now considered antisocial and inefficient (Figure 2.2c).

Antisocial because it occupies twice as much space as necessary in the radio frequency spectrum. The human voice occupies a bandwidth of 2.7kHz (3,000Hz minus 300Hz) but, when used to amplitude modulate a transmitter, the resultant signal is 6kHz wide. So to avoid causing interference, another station must be at least 6kHz away, i.e. the channels must be spaced at 6kHz intervals.

Inefficient because two-thirds of the total transmitted power is contained in the carrier which does not, in itself, convey any information. The remaining one-third of the power is distributed equally between the two sidebands, both of which convey the same information. Therefore, only one sixth of the total transmitted power actually conveys information! Imagine sending someone two copies of a message in a strong cardboard box! For example, a 150-watt AM transmitter actually transmits only 25 watts of information.

Single Sideband (J3E)

How much better would it be if the whole transmitter power of, say, 150 watts could be concentrated into one of the sidebands? Not only would it be more efficient but the transmitted bandwidth would be only 2.7kHz, the same as the baseband, enabling a doubling of channels 'at a stroke' and no power would be wasted in transmitting the carrier.

This is now possible and most communication services transmit a *single sideband* without the carrier, called J3E. The generation of a single sideband is done in three stages: firstly, amplitude modulation is carried out in the normal way producing a carrier and two sidebands. The second stage is to reject the carrier by a filtration process and finally the unwanted sideband is also filtered out, leaving just the required sideband. (Stages one and two are usually carried out simultaneously in a circuit called a balanced modulator.) To avoid wasting power, modulation is carried out at a low power level. After the carrier and unwanted sideband have been rejected by filtration, the required sideband is amplified and passed to the aerial (antenna) for transmission. The particular sideband which is transmitted is technically immaterial but the marine world decided to change from AM to SSB using the upper sideband (USB) on 1st January, 1972. This doubled the number of available MF and HF channels by decreasing the channel spacing from 6kHz to 3kHz and allowed much more effective use of transmitter power (Figure 2.3). (On the same date, the number of VHF channels was also doubled to 55 by decreasing the channel spacing from 50kHz to 25kHz; see Chapter 6.) Most other R/T services also use USB.

The one sideband is able to 'support' itself without a carrier because it is a band of radio frequencies. Although it is still necessary to generate a carrier within the transmitter for modulation purposes, it is not necessary to actually transmit the carrier! Having done its job of converting a band of *audio* frequencies into a band of *radio* frequencies by frequency addition, it is a waste of power actually to transmit the carrier.

Introduction of SSB

The change-over from AM to SSB was not easy because the two systems are incompatible to the extent that an AM receiver cannot receive an SSB transmission. Just as a carrier is necessary in the transmitter to achieve modulation, i.e., to transpose the baseband into the radio frequency part of the spectrum by frequency addition, a *re-inserted carrier* must also be generated in the corresponding receiver for *demodulation* to retranspose the upper sideband back into the audio frequency part of the spectrum by frequency subtraction. As AM receivers do not incorporate a carrier reinsertion oscillator, they cannot demodulate (detect) SSB transmissions.

The difference in technology between AM and SSB is so great that an AM set cannot be modified for SSB; it is cheaper to throw the old set away and build anew! A ten year period was set aside to complete the change over and since 1st January, 1982, SSB has been mandatory for all MF and HF marine radio installations (Figure 2.3).

Compatible SSB (H3E)

For the ten years between 1972 and 1982, most ships continued to use AM but an increasing number started using SSB. As AM and SSB are incompatible, a compatible mode of transmission, H3E, was adopted for this 10-year transitional period. Otherwise, half the World's ships would have been unable to talk to the others! A full carrier was transmitted in addition to the upper sideband to enable reception of SSB by old AM receivers (see Figure 2.4). Until 1999, H3E was mandatory and automatic on 2182kHz for compatibility with ship's lifeboat radios. Although H3E is no longer used, it may still be automatically selected on 2182kHz by some GMDSS transceivers. On these sets, J3E

should be manually programmed on 2182kHz. Selecting H3E on other frequencies switches the receiver section to AM for domestic broadcast reception.

Pilot-Carrier (R3E)

Just as a carrier is necessary for modulation purposes in the transmitter (remember, a radio frequency is added to the baseband to produce the upper sideband), a carrier (or, more correctly, a *re-inserted carrier*) must be generated within the receiver for demodulation purposes. This re-inserted carrier is then subtracted from the upper sideband to produce the original baseband frequencies. A problem lies in the fact that the receiver's re-inserted carrier must exactly match the frequency of the other station's transmitter several hundred or even several thousand miles away! While this is easy on paper, in the real world there is no such thing as plus-and-minus nothing; electronic equipment has manufacturing tolerances just like everything else. Consequently, although the transmitting station may have selected a frequency of, say, 2.0MHz, it will not be exactly 2.0MHz; it will be plus or minus a small amount.

The same applies to the receiving station's re-inserted carrier. Thus, although audio frequencies will be received, they will not be the same baseband frequencies as the input of the other station's transmitter. Consider, for example, a single 1,000Hz tone at the input of a transmitter tuned to a nominal frequency of 2.0MHz. If the transmitter's carrier is only 100Hz high, the actual carrier frequency will be 2.0001MHz. When this is added to the tone, the actual transmitted frequency will be 2.0011MHz. If the receiving station's re-inserted carrier is only 100Hz low, the actual re-inserted carrier frequency will be 1.9999MHz. When this is subtracted from the transmitted frequency, the result is 1,200Hz. Although this is an audio frequency, it is not the same audio frequency that was put into the transmitter. If this example of a single audio frequency is applied to a baseband

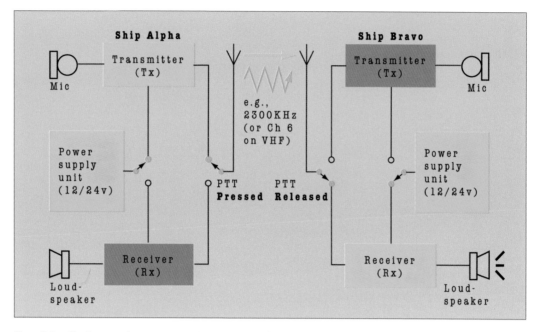

Figure 2.6 Simplex operation: one way at a time on the same frequency

(which is someone's voice), the effect is to raise the pitch of the received voice by 200Hz. The received voice could be raised (or lowered) to the extent of rendering it unintelligible.

Clarifier Control

The problem is solved by providing the receiver with a very, very, very fine tuning control which tunes the receiver's re-inserted carrier to exactly that of the other station's transmitter. The effect is to clarify (make clear) the received signal so the control is usually named 'clarifier' or 'clarity'. Clarifiers usually have a range of plus and minus 150Hz but some sets have *receiver incremental tuning* (RIT) in 10Hz steps.

Sometimes it can be difficult to judge when the clarifier control is set correctly; only the pitch of the other person's voice can be judged and this may not be known. To help, the other person may, on request, transmit a *pilot carrier* (R3E) signal. As the name implies, a very small carrier is transmitted with the upper sideband. The strength of this

pilot carrier is too small to achieve demodulation in the receiver so carrier re-insertion must still be done (by switching the receiver to 'SSB' mode). If the frequency of the re-inserted carrier does not exactly match that of the pilot carrier, a whistle is heard. So for perfect tuning, the clarifier need only be turned until the whistle stops (see Figure 2.5).

These different modes of transmission may be recalled by the following *aides memoire*:

> **A3E** could (it doesn't, but it could) **stand for ALL the signal**
> **J3E** could (it doesn't, but it could) **stand for JUST the sideband**
> **R3E** could (it doesn't, but it could) **stand for a REDUCED carrier,** and
> **H3E** could (it doesn't, but it could) **stand for the WHOLE carrier!**

Simplex Operation

Any radio communication station must

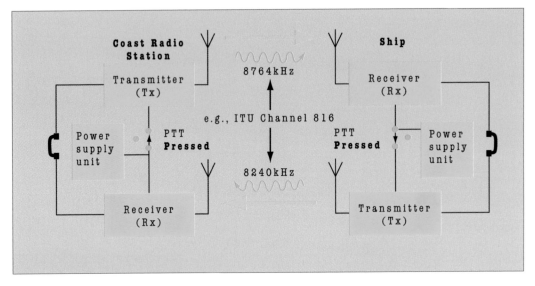

Figure 2.7   Duplex operation: simultaneous transmission and reception on different frequencies

obviously comprise a transmitter and receiver, both of which require an aerial (antenna). Fortunately, the one aerial will usually do both the transmitting or receiving jobs but not both at the same time. If only one aerial is available, it must be switched between the transmitter and receiver by means of a *press to talk* (PTT) switch. This means the equipment, also, may only be used for transmitting (talking) or receiving (listening), which requires co-ordination between mouth and thumb. This mode of operation, known as *simplex*, requires the cooperation of the other operator who must appreciate that his correspondent's ears are switched off during transmission. With this mode, both transmitters and receivers may operate on the same frequency although it is not unusual for two separate frequencies to be used (see Figure 2.6).

Duplex Operation

Simplex operation works well between skilled operators as found on ships, and at coastguard stations and harbours, but can cause problems when connected into a telephone line ashore through a Coast Radio Station. In any case, the correspondent ashore

does not have a press-to-talk switch in the telephone handset; most would not know what to do with if there was! In these situations, it is highly desirable (but not essential) to be able to talk and listen simultaneously. This can be done by using suitable equipment and two aerials/antennae; one for the transmitter and an entirely separate one for the receiver. To avoid interference between one's own transmitter and receiver, the two aerials/antennae must be spaced as far apart as possible and two separate and widely-spaced frequencies used (Figure 2.7). As Coast Radio Stations exist, principally, to handle public telephone calls, they always and only operate on a two-frequency basis. On the HF and VHF bands, the paired transmitting and receiving frequencies are selected as one 'channel' (e.g., Table 6.1, Chapter 6). On MF, the separate transmitting and receiving frequencies are selected after discussion with the Coast Radio Station operator on 2182kHz.

Duplex operation is more convenient than simplex because the press-to-talk (PTT) switch may be held depressed throughout the whole conversation without the necessity of saying 'over'. To avoid acoustic feedback,

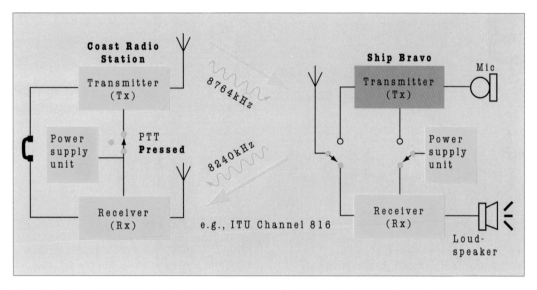

Figure 2.8   Two-frequency simplex (semi-duplex): alternate transmission and reception on two frequencies

loudspeakers cannot be used in duplex operation. Only telephone handsets which incorporate a PTT switch may be used so these are supplied as standard with duplex equipment.

NOTE: Duplex sets can also operate in the simplex mode for talking to other ships, harbours, etc. on a single frequency.

Semi-Duplex

The term is really a misnomer to describe the situation in which a small vessel with a simplex-only transceiver (a combined transmitter and receiver sharing controls, circuitry and case) is communicating with a duplex-equipped shore station. In this case, the whole operation must be conducted in the simplex mode with the co-operation of the correspondent ashore. As two frequencies are still being used, this mode is properly called *two-frequency simplex* (see Figure 2.8).

3

The Radio Spectrum

For convenience, the range of radio frequencies (being much greater than the range of audio frequencies) is sub-divided into much smaller groups or bands according to their comparative frequencies. There are no natural divisions; these are purely arbitrary, man-made divisions starting with Very Low Frequencies (VLF) then progressing through Low Frequencies (LF), Medium Frequencies (MF), High Frequencies (HF), Very High Frequencies (VHF), Ultra High Frequencies (UHF) and Super High Frequencies (SHF) to Extremely High Frequencies (EHF). There is one, as yet un-named, band of even higher frequencies before the Infra-Red band is reached. For what it is worth, the author suggests that this final band could be termed FHF (Fantastically High Frequencies), IHF (Incredibly High Frequencies) or THF (Tremendously High Frequencies). Perhaps the latter is more appropriate since the frequencies are in Terahertz (THz). As the history of radio engineering has been one of ever-increasing frequencies, the bands could be dated starting with VLF in the 1890s to THF in the 21st. century see Figure 3.1a).

VLF, 3–30kHz (1kHz = 1,000Hz)

Theoretically, the limits of the VLF band are 3 kHz to 30kHz but, since the lower frequencies are actually audio frequencies, the practical limits of VLF are 10kHz to 30kHz, making it a very narrow band indeed. Neither can these frequencies be modulated. For modulation, the radio carrier must be at least ten times the highest modulation frequency. So, as the highest speech frequency is 3kHz, the lowest radio frequency must be 30kHz. However, frequencies above 10kHz will propagate (spread) so this limits the VLF band to continuous wave (CW) systms such as navigational aids (OMEGA) and telegraphy signals.

LF, 30kHz – 300kHz

The lower frequencies are also used for navigational aids such as Decca (70–130kHz) and Loran (**LO**ng **R**ange **A**id to **N**avigation) on 100kHz. The higher frequencies are used for national long wave broadcasting (148.5–285kHz).

MF, 300kHz–3MHz (1 MHz = 1,000kHz)

The lower frequencies (190-535kHz) are used for radio beacons. An important world-wide Maritime Safety Information service, NAVTEX, uses this band. The main frequency is 518kHz but a secondary frequency, 490kHz, is also increasingly being used (see Chapter 11). The central part is used for Medium Wave regional broadcasting: 531-1602kHz (in 9kHz steps) in Europe; 530-1,700kHz (in 10kHz steps) in North America. Marine

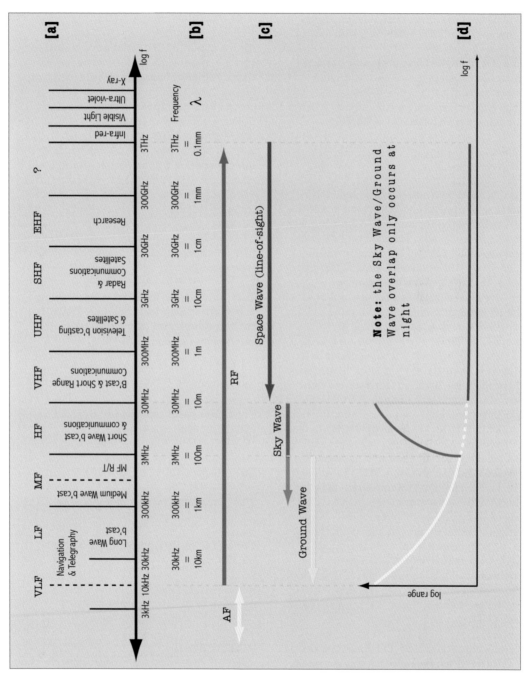

Figure 3.1   The radio spectrum showing frequencies, wavelengths, modes of propagation and ranges. **Notes:** (1) The frequency axis is drawn to a logarithmic scale to conserve space; each band is actually 10 times wider than the one on its left! (2) The overlap between the ground wave and sky wave modes of propagation (pale blue arrow) is explained more fully in Chapter 4

Radiotelephony (R/T) occupies the higher frequencies of 1606.5-2850kHz with the Distress frequency on 2182kHz. (In the USA, this is termed the Coastal Harbor Service.) Parts of this range are shared with other services such as Radio Amateurs (1.8–2.0MHz), aircraft and Standard Frequency transmissions on 2.5MHz.

HF, 3–30MHz

As this band gives ranges of several thousand miles with comparatively low power (100W+) by means of the sky wave it is, obviously, very attractive to all radio services, e.g. broadcasting, military, aviation, amateurs, marine, etc. Unfortunately, there is not room for everyone so, every few years, an international conference takes place at which the HF band is 'carved up' among the various services. However, as the higher HF frequencies tend to give longer ranges than the lower HF frequencies, all services are allocated several different 'slots' distributed throughout the band, so that each service gets six or eight small bands. For example, the Maritime Mobile Service is allocated slots around 4, 6, 8, 12, 16, 18, 22 & 25MHz. (In the USA, this is called the High Seas Service.) Each band is sub-divided into numbered channels similar to Marine VHF but with the channels spaced at 3kHz intervals. Most of them are two-frequency (duplex) channels with separate transmit and receive frequencies for communication with Coast Radio Stations but there are a few single-frequency channels for intership communication. Also within the HF band are Weatherfax and standard frequency transmissions on 5.0, 10.0, 15.0 and 20.0MHz (see Chapter 11).

Note: Before 1 July 1991, the spacing was 3.1kHz so all 'synthesised' HF sets supplied before then must be re-programmed with the new frequencies and older sets fitted with new crystals. In most cases, the set must be returned to the dealer for this work to be carried out (see ALRS Vol. 1, App. 16).

VHF, 30–300MHz

Above about 30MHz, radio waves travel in straight lines (more-or-less) so range on Earth is limited by the Earth's curvature (see Figure 1.1 & Chapter 6). Most short range services such as broadcasting, aviation, military, amateurs, private mobile radio (PMR) such as taxis, police, ambulance, fire service and shipping share this band. The International Maritime Mobile (IMM) band covers 156–162MHz with an extension to 174MHz for private channels. See Chapter 6 for more details.

UHF, 300MHz–3GHz (1 gigahertz = 1,000 megahertz)

This band is used for short-range military communications, colour TV (500–800MHz), cellular telephones (around 900MHz) & satellite TV (around 1,250MHz).

SHF, 3–30GHZ

The main use for this band is for radar and communication satellites.

EHF, 30–300GHZ

This band is the subject of ongoing research.

THF, 300GHz–3THz (1 terahertz = 1,000 gigahertz)

No doubt this band will be the subject of research in the 21st century.

WAVELENGTH

Although radio transmissions are designated by frequency, it is necessary to measure aerials (antennae) by wavelength to obtain a physical dimension. So what is the relationship between frequency and wavelength? Refer to Figure 3.2a which

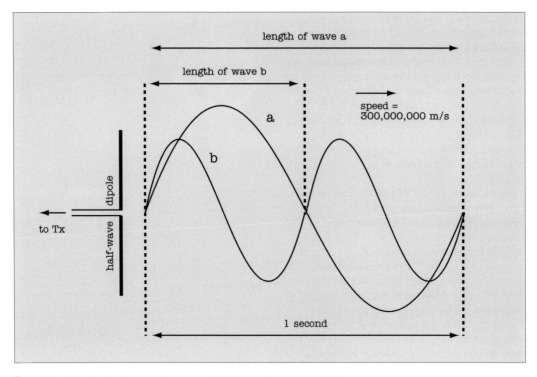

Figure 3.2   Wavelengths of one cycle per second (a) & two cycles per second (b)

shows one cycle of alternating current. This diagram also represents a radio wave emanating from the mid-point of the aerial. Since the energy is electromagnetic radiation, just like light, it travels at the speed of light, i.e., almost 300,000,000 (300 million) metres per second. So, if the wave is leaving the aerial at 300 million metres per second and it takes one second to complete one cycle, how long is the wave? Answer: 300 million metres!

Now consider Figure 3.2b which shows a radio wave of two cycles per second. Obviously, since two 'wiggles' are now being packed into one second, the wavelength must be halved, i.e. 150 million metres.

So we see that wavelength is inversely proportional to frequency – as frequency increases, wavelength decreases. The formula is:

$$\lambda = 300,000,000 \div \text{Frequency}$$

and Frequency $= 300,000,000 \div \lambda$

(where λ = wavelength). (Or $\lambda = 300 \div$ MHz and MHz $= 300 \div \lambda$.) See also Figure 3.1b.

Obviously, 2Hz is an exaggerated example. But if the frequency was 2MHz, the wavelength must be 150 metres. This is the wavelength of MF R/T, the significance of which will become apparent in Chapter 5.

1,000Hz = 1 kilohertz (kHz)
    [one thousand]
1,000kHz = 1 megahertz (MHz)
    [one million]
1,000MHz = 1 gigahertz (GHz)
    [one thousand million]
1,000GHz = 1 terahertz (THz)
    [one billion (Englsh)]

MODES OF PROPAGATION

Very low, low and medium frequencies follow

the curvature of the Earth and consequently, for any given frequency, the range is determined by the amount of power transmitted. The wave is diffracted (bent) because the lower end of the wave penetrates the surface of the Earth to a depth of a few metres. As the bottom of the wave travels slightly slower through the Earth's surface than the top does through the atmosphere, the wavefront becomes tilted causing it to 'stick' to the Earth's surface.

As the transmitted frequency is increased, the depth of penetration decreases thus causing less bending. Additionally, the amount of energy absorbed by the Earth's surface and atmosphere also increases with increasing frequency. Thus, for a given amount of power, range is inversely proportional to frequency but, for a given frequency, range is proportional to power. This is why long waves are used for national broadcasting whereas medium waves are used for regional broadcasting. By day, the Marine MF band gives a maximum range of 300 miles with the maximum allowed power of 400 watts.

Frequencies above 3MHz do not penetrate the Earth so, without diffraction, the range on the ground becomes 'line of sight'. However, waves between 3MHz and 30MHz (HF band) are 'reflected' off the ionosphere high above the Earth to give ranges of several thousand miles (see Chapter 4). At this stage it is sufficient to state that within the HF band, range increases with increasing frequency.

4

Short Wave Propagation

As we saw earlier, short waves propagate mainly by sky waves via the ionosphere and so give very long ranges. However, the situation is not quite as straightforward as depicted in Figure 1.3.

Although the ionosphere is shown as one neat layer for simplicity, at times there can be four layers designated D, E, F1 & F2 working outwards from the Earth (see Figure 4.1). Despite being identical in nature, all four layers have slightly different characteristics.

D Layer This, the lowest at 30–50 miles above the Earth, exists only during the day: from about a quarter of an hour after sunrise to a quarter of an hour before sunset in the Tropics and temperate zones. In the depth of temperate Winters, this interval can increase to an hour or more depending on latitude. It does not refract (bend) radio waves but absorbs all energy below about 3MHz.

E Layer This layer is strongly ionized during the day and remains weakly ionized at night. At 60–90 miles, its height is almost twice that of the D Layer. It refracts (bends) radio waves from about 4MHz to 8MHz during the day but from 100kHz to 4MHz at night due to the absence of the 'D' Layer.

F1 Layer This layer, too, is strongly ionized during the day and exists at a height between 90 and 150 miles – nearly twice that of the E layer. It refracts radio waves of between about 8–16MHz.

F2 Layer This is also strongly ionized by day and refracts radio waves of between about 16–30MHz. Its height is between about 150 and 250 miles in summer but a little lower in winter.

Important Note

On HF, here are two general rules for initial assessment of the OTF/OWF:
1. The greater the range required, the greater the frequency required.
2. Sun high (day), frequency high; Sun low (night), frequency low (about half the day frequency).

When tuning Telex (F1B) stations, it is vitally important to understand the way in which voice and Telex signals are published. Voice signals are listed as their suppressed carrier and this is set on the receiver's display. In the example given on p. 26, 8761kHz is that of Ostend's suppressed carrier. Select 8761kHz on the dial and Ostend Radio is heard. Telex frequencies, however, are listed as the centre of their transmitted bandwidth, termed the 'assigned' frequency. This is offset from the suppressed carrier by +1.7kHz. To receive Telex signals correctly with an SSB receiver set to USB, this offset of +1.7kHz must be subtracted from the listed frequency. In the example

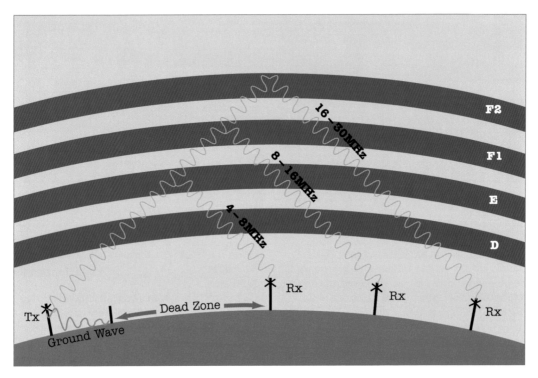

Figure 4.1   Daytime situation, showing how the highest frequency gives the greatest range

Important Note continued

of Ostend, their Telex frequency is listed as 8435.5kHz. To receive this frequency correctly, a USB receiver must be tuned to 8435.5-1.7 = 8433.8kHz. No signal will be heard by a receiver tuned to 8435.5kHz!

(Purely for assessing band conditions, 1kHz or 1.5kHz is much more easily subtracted from Telex frequencies.)

Coast Radio Stations will happily supply details of their own services but full details of all Coast Radio Stations worldwide are published in the Admiralty List of Radio Signals (ALRS), Volume 1. Part 1 covers Europe, Africa and most of Asia; Part 2 covers the rest of the World. They are available from Admiralty Chart Agents at all major ports worldwide.

For leisure sailors, the Admiralty now publishes a new compendium of marine radio services for popular sailing areas. 'Admiralty Maritime Communications' is

Important Note continued

in three volumes covering the British Isles and the Mediterannean including the Azores and Canaries (NP289), the Azores, Canaries, Gibraltar and the Caribbean (NP290) and the British Isles and Baltic States (NP291). These are republished every two years but free updates to them and ALRS are available in the weekly 'Notices To Mariners' at Admiralty Chart Agents or the UKHO website: www.ukho.gov.uk

Admiralty publications and thousands of other nautical books, both new and second-hand, are obtainable by post from the Warsash Nautical Bookshop, 6, Dibbles Road, Warsash, Southampton, SO31 9HZ, U.K., Telephone: +44 (0)1489 572 384. Facsimile: +44 (0)1489 885 756.

Email: orders@nauticalbooks.co.uk, Website: www.nauticalbooks.co.uk. A free list is updated quarterly.

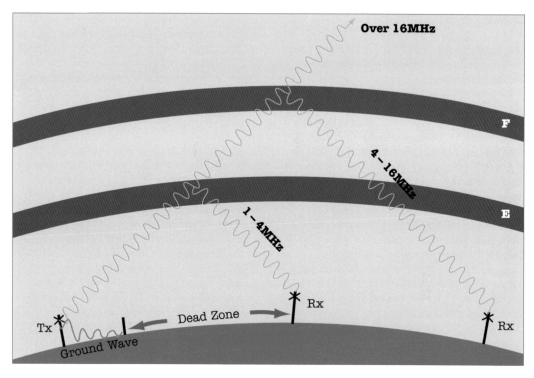

Figure 4.2   The night-time situation, showing how the same range is achieved by much lower frequencies

DIURNAL (DAY/NIGHT) VARIATION

At night, the ionospheric situation is very different because the layers are formed by intense UV radiation from the sun which disappears at night! However, the layers do not go completely at sunset; the E Layer remains weakly ionized and the two F Layers combine to form one F Layer roughly mid-way between the two day-time layers. Thus, at night, there are only two layers, E and F (Figure 4.2).

The greatest effect is due to the disappearance of the D Layer which completely absorbs energy below 3MHz. The E Layer can refract radio waves in the MF band but, during the day, these are unable to reach the E Layer. At night, the medium frequencies are able to be refracted by the E Layer, so the range of MF R/T is greatly increased by virtue of the sky wave. So, by day, MF range is a function of power to a maximum of 300 miles with 400 watts. At night, however, ranges of 1,000 miles or more are easily possible! (This explains the ground-wave/skywave overlap in Figure 3.1c.)

Short Waves at Night

The HF band is also affected at night because the two F Layers combine and are much less strongly ionized. The effect is to reduce the maximum frequency which can be refracted by a factor of about two. Thus, whatever has been found to be the best 'slot' by day, the frequency must be reduced to about half that at night. For example, if the 16MHz band was being used by day, the 8MHz band will be found best at night.

Seasonal Variation

Just as the sun's intensity (and therefore the ionosphere) varies greatly between day and night, outside the Tropics there is also a seasonal variation between summer and winter which affects the choice of frequency.

Latitude Variation

The sun's intensity (and the ionosphere) also varies greatly with latitude and affects the choice of frequency.

Sunspot Variation

If an image of the sun is projected onto a sheet of white paper (Danger – do not look at the sun directly, even with dark glasses) a number of black specks are seen and the number varies daily. These are sunspots – phenomena which have remained a mystery since man started counting them about 3,000 years ago. These records show that the average number varies sinusoidally (our old friend the sine wave, again) with peaks occurring at 11.1 year cycles. Sunspots have a profound effect on HF propagation, being helpful at sunspot peaks and detrimental during sunspot troughs.

Optimum Traffic/Working Frequency (OTF/OWF)

Use of the highest HF frequencies involves utilization of the highest (F2) ionospheric layer which produces the greatest range. (Putting the 'mirror' further away gives the greatest distance covered on Earth). This is the reason behind the brief statement earlier that 'the higher the frequency, the greater the range'. So, why not use the highest frequencies all the time? Reference to Fig. 4.1 shows that between the end of the fairly short ground wave coverage and the start of the sky wave coverage, there exists a dead zone or zone of silence. Thus the frequency and, therefore, the range could be too great! The trick (or, rather, skill of the operator) is to use the most appropriate frequency for the distance to be covered taking all the variable factors into consideration.

Considerable research is undertaken continuously by a number of organizations throughout the World and frequency prediction charts are available from the companies providing HF services three months in advance. Alternatively, listen to the regular Traffic Lists broadcast from the Coast Radio Station of choice or those nearby. Straddle the most likely frequency with the ones next above and below, note the band giving best reception then use that band for the next hour or so.

Many of the more important HF stations also handle Telex traffic. Even if Telex is not fitted, a useful trick is to listen to their continuous channel-free call-signs on the various Telex bands. This is an instant measure of propagation conditions and gives a good indication of the best R/T Band to use as the frequencies are very similar. Example: if OST (Morse: – – – • • • –) from Ostend Radio is heard strongly on 8434kHz, it is a good indication that ITU Channel 815 (ship transmits on 8237kHz and receives on 8761kHz) is the best R/T channel to communicate through Ostend Radio for at least the next hour.(Important: **see the** **on pages 23 & 24.**)

'Multihop' Propagation

The greatest distance which can be covered in one 'hop' is about 2,500 miles (4,000km). The signal can then be reflected back into the Ionosphere to be refracted and reflected several times to encircle the world - going both ways!

S.I.D.s and Magnetic Storms (Radio 'Blackouts')

Although different in nature, the unpredictable effect of sudden Ionospheric disturbances (SIDs) and magnetic storms (products of an unstable Sun) is to cause a radio 'blackout' for several hours - even up to a day. The only answer to this problem is to communicate by satellite (see Chapter 10).

5

Licensing & Installation

A vessel must be licensed for R/T installation and the set must always be controlled by an operator who is authorised by the government with whom the vessel is registered, i.e. the vessel's flag. For a vessel to be licensed, the equipment must be approved by the government of the flag under which the vessel sails. This is most important since, in addition to a high international standard, each maritime government can (and does) superimpose its own national standard on the construction of marine radio equipment and the standards vary greatly. To be legal, therefore, the set should be bought in the country under whose flag the yacht sails. It is very galling for Britons to have to pay almost twice the price in Britain for what appears to be the identical Japanese-made set in New York or Singapore! The situation is very similar to the legal requirements for motor vehicles where the vehicle must be licensed annually and the

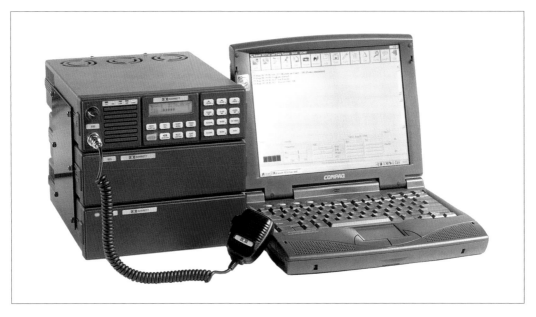

A modern HF transceiver coupled to a laptop

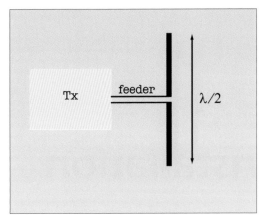

Figure 5.1   Classic half-wave dipole about 3ft at 150MHz, but 246ft at 2MHz! No Earth required

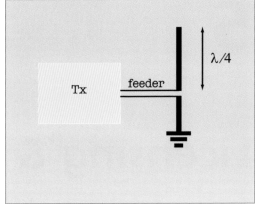

Figure 5.2   Quarter-wave monopole: about 123ft at 2MHz. Earth used as the lower half of the half-wave dipole

driver (operator) must be trained and qualified by examination. However, anyone may use the set under the supervision of the authorised operator. Similarly in exactly the same way that a vehicle is allocated a registration number when first licensed, the vessel is also allocated a unique registration number (the call sign) for identification purposes. Ship's licences, which must be renewed annually are bought over the counter or through the post from a government department or agency (free from FCC in USA); operator's certificates, which are valid for life, are usually awarded upon successful examination for which a fee is payable (also free in USA).

There are several grades of operator certificate; the relevant one for voluntarily-equipped vessels is called the 'Restricted' certificate. The full title varies from country to country. Throughout Europe (which includes UK) it is called a CEPT Long Range Radiotelephone Operator's Certificate. By including GMDSS techniques and frequencies, it is superior to the ITU 'Restricted' certificate. In Australia it's a Restricted Certificate of Proficiency; in the USA it's a Restricted Radiotelephone Operator Permit. Don't worry about that word 'restricted'. It means that the operator is restricted to approved marine (i.e. not

aeronautical or Amateur) transmitters which will only transmit on pre-set marine frequencies.

The UK overall radio regulatory authority is the Radiocommunications Agency (RA) which merged with OFCOM in late-2003. Ship's licences are handled by the Radio Licensing Centre, Bristol and examinations for the Long Range Certificate are conducted by the Association of Marine Electronics and Radio Colleges (AMERC) following training at a centre approved by the Maritime and Coastguard Agency (MCA). Addresses at the end of this book.

The ship's licence and operator's certificate must be available for inspection by an authorised government officer at any port of call. Ideally, the ship's licence should be displayed near the radio installation. British yachts are given an annual licence disc, very similar to a motor tax disc, for display in a cabin or wheelhouse window. A plastic licence holder is supplied for this purpose.

NOTE:
Before entering the territorial waters of any country, ALRS, Volume 1 should be consulted for regulations on the local use of radio.

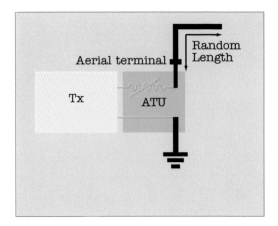

Figure 5.3   Short random length of wire used with earth and ATU to 'make up' the aerial to quarter-wavelength

INSTALLATION

Ideally, this should be carried out by a marine electronics specialist but a DIY installation is feasible provided that particular attention is paid to the power, aerial/antenna and earth installation. Modern marine SSBs fall into two styles: two unit and three unit. The distinction is caused by the fact that there are three major units to a communications transceiver: the electronics, the controls and an aerial/antenna tuning unit (ATU). In the (good?) old days when electrons were kept in glass bottles (valves/tubes), all three units were housed in one big box but there are advantages in separating them. The choice is influenced by the space available. So, what is an ATU and why do we need one?

AERIAL TUNING UNIT (ATU)

An ATU is needed because the basic transmitting aerial is a half wave dipole (that is, it is exactly half a wavelength in length) for maximum efficiency. This is why it is necessary to be able to convert frequency to wavelength (see Figures 5.1 and 3.2).

On the Marine VHF band, this causes no problem because the wavelength works out at 300 ÷ 156.8MHz (Channel 16) = 1.9m

(approx). Therefore, the aerial should be about 0.95m (about 37.5 in) overall from tip to tip. As the energy radiates mostly at right angles to the physical plane of the aerial, it should be mounted vertically and at least 5 wavelengths (about 9.5m) above the Earth for all-round radiation. With most mobile installations, the arrangement of Figure 5.1 is awkward so an electrical 'fiddle' is arranged whereby the two quarter-wave halves of the aerial are joined together to form one continuous half wavelength and the connections made at one end – usually the lower end. The 'fiddle' is necessary because, like any other electrical circuit, two connections are required but there is only one (top or bottom) end! (Not a concern for the operator luckily; this is an engineering problem). So, no problem for a yacht on the Marine VHF band.

The problem arises when the transmit frequency is lowered to HF or MF. On the MF R/T band of approximately 2MHz, the wavelength is 300 ÷ 2 = 150m, giving a required aerial length of 75m which is 246 feet (vertically), ideally at a height of about 2,500 feet! Obviously this is not feasible, not even ashore. So, on the lower frequencies, a compromise must be accepted. Fortunately, the first compromise causes very little loss of efficiency. If a good electrical connection can be made to the Earth, it can be used as the lower half of the half-wave dipole to form an 'earth return'. This reduces the aerial proper to a quarter-wave monopole (or unipole). See Figure 5.2. However, this still means an aerial length of 123 feet, although it may now be supported on (but insulated from) the surface of the Earth (or deck). Feasible ashore but still very difficult at sea and therefore rarely seen. A pirate radio ship is an example of this arrangement.

For a shoreside example, the photograph shows a typical Coast Radio Station. The thin lattice masts, called 'mast radiators', are the actual quarter-wave aerials; the wires are merely supporting the masts and are double-insulated to prevent absorption of radio energy. Similar arrangements can be seen at

A Coast Radio Station

local domestic broadcasting stations. For most users, however, a further compromise must be accepted and this next one does reduce efficiency.

The transmitter must have, or 'think' it has, a quarter wavelength of conductor (wire) connected to its output stage. So, if the full quarter wavelength cannot be erected, the transmitter must be fooled into thinking that it has the required length. In other words, if the aerial is not physically one quarter wavelength long, it must be made electrically one quarter wavelength. The trick is to throw out as much wire as is possible and as vertical as possible and coil the rest up somewhere (Figure 5.3).

This 'make-weight' aerial is called the Aerial (or Antenna) Tuning Unit (ATU) and must be made variable to accommodate the different lengths of aerial required for different frequencies. For example, if 123 feet is required and a 7.1m (23 feet) glass-fibre whip is being used, an effective length of 100 feet must be coiled up somewhere. Since the most effective part of the aerial is at the bottom, it can be seen that on the lower frequencies at least, a short whip is very inefficient. There is nothing magical about a GRP whip; it is merely a length of copper wire encased in a GRP tube for support. However, 'loaded' whips, with spirally-wound wire to accommodate greater length, are more efficient on the MF and lower HF bands.

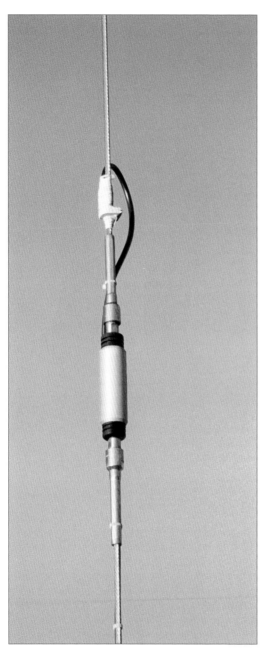

A lower backstay insulator showing the method of making the aerial connection

Motorboats with very short masts have little choice but to use them.

Sailing yachts fare much better by using part of the rigging, usually the backstay, to act as the aerial as it is usually the longest piece of wire on a sailboat. Although it is, usually, stainless steel which has poor conductivity compared with copper and is not vertical, it is nevertheless far superior to a whip. If a mizzen backstay or cap shroud can be linked to the triatic of a yawl or ketch, so much the better. On a large sailing yacht, the backstay (plus triatic?) could be longer than a quarter wavelength at the higher end of the HF band.

Most (but not all) ATUs have provision for electrically shortening the aerial. The operating manual will stipulate the minimum and maximum lengths of aerial which may be used (the minimum is usually 23 feet (7.1m) which is the size of the smallest whip). Obviously, those parts of the rigging acting as the aerial must be insulated from the yacht itself and a connection made by heavily insulated copper wire (not coaxial cable) from the ATU's aerial terminal to a point just above the bottom insulator. This in turn should be about 6 feet (2m) above deck level for safety (Figure 5.4). A 'trick-of-the-trade' is to use the braided sheath only of coaxial cable threaded through plastic water pipe which is formed into a loop at the top to prevent ingress of water. The braided sheath of the cable is then secured to the backstay with a stainless-steel hose clip. The plastic water-pipe is then led through a deck gland, formed into a loop and brought up to the aerial insulator at the top of the ATU just beneath the deck-head. The top insulator should be 12–18 inches (0.5m) down from the masthead. The ATU is connected between the output of the transmitter and the aerial to tune the aerial to be electrically one quarter wavelength. With single unit sets, where the (manual) ATU is incorporated into the transmitter, there could be several yards of wasted 'aerial' running horizontally and close to the water between the set mounted near the chart table and the aerial proper. A big advantage of the two-unit or three-unit sets, where the automatic ATU is separate, is that it can be placed immediately beneath the backstay or whip aerial for greatest

An ATU, HF set combo from Barrett Communications. The ATU is the box on top

efficiency. Two-unit sets have the controls on the front of the electronics box and a separate automatic ATU but this still means that space has to be found at the chart table for the box of electronics. This snag is overcome with the very latest three-unit sets which have a small, lightweight control box which is easily positioned at the chart table, a separate box for the electronics which can be tucked away under a berth or at the bottom of a locker near the battery and an automatic ATU.

Remember: the ATU must be adjusted (manually or automatically) every time the transmit frequency is changed – as the required length of aerial must be changed with the change of frequency. With manual tuning, the correct point is indicated by maximum reading on the aerial current meter; with automatic ATUs, just press the tune button.

There is a very slight advantage in using an ATU between the aerial and the receiver, but the advantage is so small that it is uneconomic to bother in most cases. However, in tranceivers, since an ATU is needed for the transmitter section, it is arranged that the ATU is used for reception as well.

Note: As an alternative to the rather expensive ATU, a much cheaper 'antenna coupler' may be offered. This is purely a safety device presenting a 50Ω load to the transmitter. It will not improve the efficiency of the aerial, as will a proper ATU, and should not be considered for serious use.

The same principles inevitably apply to a VHF set – which also contains an ATU. However, it is set for Channel 16 as the percentage change of frequency from 156.8MHz (Ch 16) to the extreme limits of 156MHz and 162MHz is so small as to make a variable ATU unnecessary.

EARTH OR GROUND

An electrical 'earth' or 'ground' may be the real surface of the planet Earth or the body of the vessel and is the neutral part of the circuit. For SSB sets, a good earth connection is absolutely vital as it is half the aerial system! (No earth is required for VHF sets as they use a stand-alone half-wave aerial.) Mariners are fortunate in having easy access to the sea which is very highly conductive and makes a superb earth. For steel and aluminium vessels, a substantial connection to the nearest frame or bulkhead will suffice but for wooden or GRP boats with transmitters up to about 150W, an earth plate of at least one square metre or yard, placed well below the waterline, is the recommended

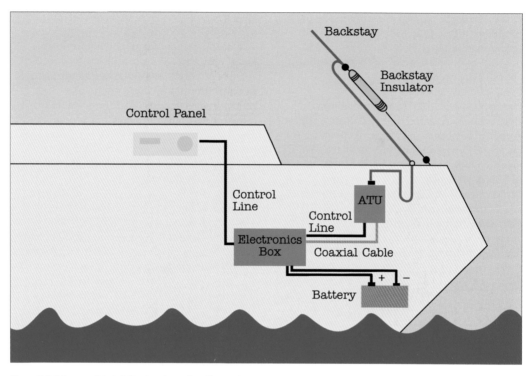

Figure 5.4 A three-unit installation in schematic sailing yacht

minimum. Some yachts are now being fitted with copper sheathing like the old tea clippers and this makes an ideal earth. Until the mid-60's, the earth plate was usually a 15cm (six-inch) wide copper strip laid the length of the boat below the waterline and secured with copper boat nails. Of course this is impractical in GRP hulls and nowadays it is usually a special earthing block (the smallest about the size of a 200gm block of chocolate) consisting of thousands of tiny metal spheres fused together. Being porous, the surface area of these spheres amounts to a square metre or more depending on the size. To prevent corrosion and for good electrical contact, they are gold plated; hence their gold-plated price! These blocks must not be painted or they will be ruined beyond redemption! Although the outer surface may become fouled, the inner surfaces will remain clean. They are supplied as a kit complete with fixing bolts and a phial of silver-loaded paint to improve the contact between bolt-head and block.

Note: the block cannot be too large; the bigger the better. Sailing yachts with large, deep keels or centreplates may use them for earthing. Even encapsulated keels can be used provided the ballast is in one solid piece. Keels made up of boiler punchings or scrap lead simply will not do. Although encapsulated keels do not make direct contact with the sea, the GRP hull acts as the dielectric of a huge capacitor formed by the ballast and sea through which the radio frequencies will penetrate. If the radio installation is planned before the GRP hull is laid up, long wide strips of perforated copper or zinc can be incorporated into the bilge area to form an 'earth mat'. Even fine mesh galvanized chicken wire will make an excellent earth if there is enough of it. The chicken wire armature (framework) of concrete boats can also be used provided all the sections are bonded together with soldered joints. With fin and skeg yachts, however, where the backstay or a transom mounted whip is being used, it may be better to use two earth blocks, one either side of the propeller, rather than a long earthing strip connecting the keel bolts. Engine blocks or propellers should not be used – they are just not big enough.

Connection to the ATU's earth terminal should be made with 50mm x 0.5mm copper tape for 150W sets or 100mm x 0.5mm tape for anything more powerful. Ordinary electrical earthing wire is inadequate. Although it may have the same cross-sectional area as the copper tape, here we are dealing with radio frequencies which do not pass through the conductor but only along the outer surface. So it is surface area which matters, not cross-sectional area

POWER SUPPLY REQUIREMENTS

Since the purpose of the transmitter is to convert direct current (DC) energy into radio frequency (RF) energy, power input is crucial to the success of an SSB set.

Most small boat SSB transceivers operate on a 12 volt system; the higher-power sets used in merchant ships are usually arranged for 24 volts for greater efficiency. It is important to realise, however, that this '12 volts' is a nominal figure; it could be anything between 11V and 15V depending on the state of charge of the battery. A lead–acid cell (a battery is made up of a number of cells) produces 2.1V when fully charged but not under charge. Thus, a '12 volt' battery, with 6 cells connected in series, should register 12.6V when not supplying current, i.e., 'open circuit'. Under charge the voltage will rise but it should not be allowed to rise above 15V. Where the charging is controlled by an automatic regulator such as in a motor vehicle or boat, charging will usually be stopped when the voltage has risen to about 13.6V or 13.8V and this is the normal operating voltage of mobile electrical equipment. Manufacturers usually make their equipment capable of accepting 11–15V without damage but radio transmitters, which are particularly sensitive to input voltage

changes, will only give their quoted output for a specific (normally 13.6V) input voltage. The output will fall dramatically for even a small reduction of input voltage. So, the battery charger (engine or generator) should be kept running all the time that the transmitter is in operation. (See 'On Board Interference' which follows.) This point is particularly important if Telex is being used as this system, being considerably more effective than speech, draws much more power. See Chapter 11.

Another very important point, often neglected, is that the quoted 13.6V (or whatever) is at the input terminals of the set. To avoid an unacceptable voltage drop, the supply lead should be in very heavy cable. If a power lead (or 'cord') is supplied, it is not intended to be extended. Consider this: a long, thin cable could easily measure 0.1Ω resistance – a very small amount which would not be noticed by a mains lawn mower at the bottom of the garden. However, on full power transmit, the average 150W SSB set draws 25 amps on peak load. According to Dr. G. S. Ohm's famous law, this results in a voltage loss of 2.5 volts along the cable, i.e., 13.6 – 2.5 = 11.1V which is verging on the inoperable! For best results, a large-capacity battery (say, 90Ah) should be placed to allow very short cables to the transmitter. This exercise shows the advantage of the three-part set where the box of electronics can be positioned close to the supply battery and the control section where convenient for operation.

It also illustrates the improved efficiency of the 24 volt system. By doubling the voltage, the current would be halved to 12.5A for the same output power. With the same cable, therefore, the voltage drop would be only 1.25V which would still leave 25.95V at the terminals of the set. Thus, a 24 volt system is four times more efficient than a 12 volt system and prudent sailors install this for radio use.

The state of charge of a lead acid battery is best tested by measuring the specific gravity (s.g.) of the electrolyte (dilute sulphuric acid) with a hydrometer. These are available cheaply at any good garage or car accessory store. A fully charged cell should register 1.26 which equates to a voltage of 2.1V. The s.g. should not be allowed to fall below 1.16 (or 1.8V per cell) which indicates a flat battery. The battery should be recharged as soon as possible after discharge; if left for more than a few days, recharge may not be possible. It is not generally appreciated that the standard automotive battery self-discharges by about 1% per day and should be recharged at least once per month whether used or not. The modern sealed batteries are much better in this respect but have the disadvantage that hydrometer testing is no longer possible and one must rely on a simple voltage check.

Warning
Lead-acid batteries give off hydrogen when being charged, which is highly explosive when mixed with air. **No smoking; no naked lights; wear gloves, goggles and protective clothing. Switch off all circuits before connecting/ disconnecting batteries.**

CHOICE OF SET - GMDSS APPROVAL.

Since 1 February 1999, Priority Alerts and Routine Calls should now be made automatically by simply pressing a Digital Selective Calling (DSC) button on a new GMDSS marine radio or DSC controller. In Europe, GMDSS approval is indicated by a 'CE' and a 'ships wheel' mark. If a traditional voice call is initially made on Ch. 16 or 2182kHz, it is increasingly less likely that anyone will hear it! New, non-GMDSS marine radios cannot now be bought in Europe although second-hand, 'type-approved', non-GMDSS marine radios are still allowed for craft under 300 tons. Until GMDSS radios become the norm, most yachts will continue to 'listen-out' on Ch.16/2182kHz. British Coastguards have stated that they will maintain a dedicated (headphone) watch on Ch.16 for the foreseeable future. Thereafter, a

general loudspeaker watch will be kept in the Operations Room.

All Coastguards and Merchant Ships now keep DSC watch on Ch.70 but many Merchant Ships still maintain a voluntary watch on Ch.16 and Ch.13 (designated for 'intership safety') also. There are, now, no dedicated Radio Officers (all radios are on the Bridge and operated by the Deck Officers), so watch is not normally kept on 2182kHz. In Area A1, DSC watch is kept on Ch.70; in A2 it is Ch.70 + 2187.5kHz and in A3/A4 it is Ch.70 + 2187.5kHz + 8414.5kHz + another HF.

On Board Interference

In addition to receiving wanted radio signals, receivers also respond to unwanted signals, called 'noise', which interfere with wanted signals and degrade reception. Noise can be natural and man-made and, in extreme cases, can completely obliterate reception of wanted signals. Some noise will be external and picked up by the aerial but some will be internally generated within the receiver itself. There is little the operator can do about natural, external noise or that generated within the set. A lot of noise, though, may come from other electrical equipment on board and this is one area in which the keen operator can do a lot to help himself at very little expense (but sometimes a lot of effort). But the improvement in radio communications well justifies the effort.

All rotating DC electrical machinery, in fact anything which makes a spark, creates electromagnetic waves which causes interference to radio receivers nearby. Fortunately, on a small boat, this is easily traced and is not too difficult or expensive to eradicate or, at least, reduce. On a calm day when well clear of land, all engines, generators and everything electrical should be switched off to create a 'dead ship'. (Filament lamps may be left burning if necessary as they do not cause radio interference but fluorescent lamps must be

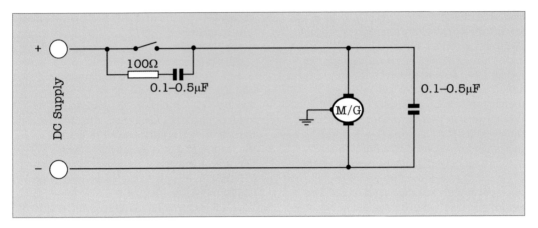

Figure 5.5a   Interference suppression, stage one: a capacitor across the bushes of a motor or generator. An additional suppressor across the contacts of a switch or thermostat helps reduce contact-wear

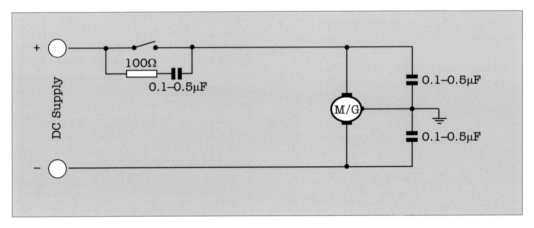

Figure 5.5b Stage two: a pair of capacitors – one between each brush and the earthed motor frame

turned off because they do.) Then a radio receiver should be switched on to the LF (long wave) band and a note made of the amount of background noise in a clear space between stations. The noise heard is the sum of the natural background noise and that generated within the set about which nothing can be done by the operator. The radio can be the main station receiver or a good domestic 'tranny'. Indeed, a portable receiver or RDF is extremely useful as it can be moved around the boat to 'sniff-out' the location of interference and the aerial used to pinpoint the source. Decca or Loran navigators can

also be used although they do take a minute or two to respond to any change. They operate on LF and usually incorporate a means of measuring the received signal-to-noise ratio on a scale of 1-9 or 1-99 so the higher the figure, the better. (Note: Philips navigators measure the amount of noise so the lower the figure the better!)

Then electrical machines (bilge pump, water pump, windscreen wipers, etc.) should be switched on one at a time, noting any device which causes a decrease in the signal-to-noise ratio. An important point worth

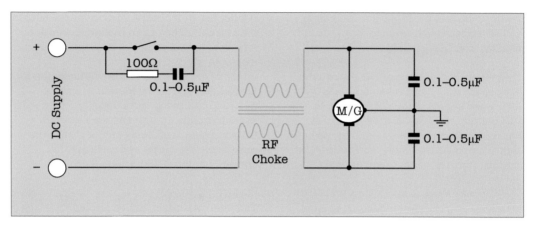

Figure 5.5c Stage three – the final solution

noting is that it may not just be the device which causes the interference but the associated switch or thermostat – and don't forget that the refrigerator unit may not start up as soon as the switch is made. By the time all electrical devices have been operated for a few minutes each and the level of interference checked, the battery will need charging so the engine or generator should then be started in neutral gear. It will usually be found that it is the charging alternator which causes most interference. Of course, there is no ignition interference from diesel engines. After a few minutes, when the battery is fully charged, the noise should reduce as the charging cutout operates. Then, finally, the propeller should be engaged. There is a possibility that the rotating prop shaft could also cause interference; they often do if allowed to trail when sailing.

Having traced the source(s) of interference, steps must now be taken to suppress it. This can be done in stages dictated by the degree of success of each stage. Firstly, a capacitor of 0.1μF to 0.5μF can be tried connected across the brush gear of the offending motor or generator. If this does not eliminate the interference, a pair of similar capacitors connected between each brush and the frame of the machine can be tried. The frame of every machine should be connected to a good earth such as the keel or earth block by a heavy gauge earth wire. The

capacitors should be connected as closely as possible to the brushes and frame. The type supplied for connecting across the points of petrol engine ignition distributors are ideal as they have a slotted lug welded to the metal case which can be trapped beneath a screw on the motor frame. They are also cheaply and readily obtainable from any car accessory shop.

If that fails, the third stage is to connect a pair of 'chokes' in series with the supply leads. These are commercially available but they must be of the type suitable for use at low frequencies. Suppressors which are effective at low frequencies are usually effective at high frequencies as well. Most of the commonly available chokes are specifically made for TV suppression and are not effective at lower frequencies. Another important point to watch is the current carrying capacity of the choke; many are made for use on mains equipment where the voltage is high but the current is very low. Even a small DC motor will draw several amps from a 12 volt supply. See Figure 5.5c.

Switches, float switches, thermostats and relays can also cause annoying, if intermittent, interference. Among the worst offenders are the relays in auto pilots which operate every few seconds. Connecting the aforementioned capacitor in series with a 100Ω resistor across the contacts of switches greatly increases the life of the contacts as well as reducing interference. The manufacturer may already have done this.

Amateur Radio shops or DIY electronic component shops may be able to help with advice and supply of these components. The best people, of course, are the specialist marine electronics dealers but they may only wish to carry out the whole work; this is the simplest (but most expensive) answer.

Radio interference from electronic computers is in a different league. Older models are particularly bad for radiating strong interference which is extremely difficult to suppress; new models are much better in this respect. Basically, the case must be shielded or screened in metal which is earthed. Experiments can be conducted with kitchen baking foil stuck onto the outside of the case although this does not look very pretty. Conductive aerosol paint is available which can be sprayed onto the inside of the case but this is a delicate job for the specialist. If Telex operation, using a personal computer, is required, it is best to have the whole equipment supplied and installed by a specialist company who will ensure that the entire system functions correctly before they present their bill.

If all this sounds like a lot of 'hassle', it is! The more electrical and electronic equipment that is carried on board, the more problems there will be and the less sailing will be done. In terms of safety and convenience, the benefits of marine radio are enormous but they have to be paid for in effort as well as cash.

6

The VHF Band and its relationship with SSB

Any boat fitted with a long-range SSB radio also needs a VHF set for local, short-range communications. With all USA-registered craft, a VHF set is mandatory if an SSB is fitted. So a chapter on VHF is relevant in this book.

VHF CHANNELS

Soon after the Second World War, the International Maritime Mobile Band was established with 28 numbered channels spaced at 50kHz intervals between 156MHz and 162MHz. With improved technology in 1972 it became possible to increase the number of channels to 55 by halving the channel spacing to 25kHz. Rather than re-number afresh, the original channel numbers were retained on the original centre-frequencies and fresh numbers allocated to the new, interleaved channels. Sadly, the new numbering sequence could not start at 29 because Channels 29-59 were already allocated for private use. The first free number available for allocation, therefore,

Simrad's DSC-enabled RD68 VHF set

The entrance lock and control tower of a marina in coastal waters. In the UK, VHF Channels 80 & 'M' are used to control traffic movements

was 60. This explains the present rather curious numbering sequence given in Table 6.1.

Channel 16 Roughly in the centre of the Band, this is designated as the Distress and Calling channel; the VHF equivalent of 2182kHz MF except that there are no Silence Periods. All other channels are designated for a specific purpose, either on an exclusive basis or, with some, a shared basis. As shore stations control communication with ships, it is only with intership communication that the ship's radio operator must choose an appropriate channel when called on Ch. 16 (the choice is made by the station called). For preference, the choice should be one of the exclusive intership channels of 6, 8, 72 and 77. There are other Intership Channels which are shared with the Port Operations Service but, obviously, they should be kept as clear as possible.

It is very important to appreciate that, out of the 55 channels, 35 of them are two-frequency ('duplex') channels, mostly reserved for 'Public Correspondence', i.e. telephone calls to the shore. It is impossible to communicate with other ships on any of these Public Correspondence channels due to the use of separate and widely-spaced transmit and receive frequencies. Although it is technically possible to communicate with other ships on any of the 20 single-frequency channels in the centre of the Band, obviously, those reserved exclusively for 'Port Operations' must not be used. See Table 6.1.

Channel 70 This used to be one of the exclusive intership channels but since 1 February 1992, it is now an exclusive Digital Selective Calling (DSC) channel for Distress and calling under the GMDSS. Speech is strictly forbidden. On the new GMDSS sets, it cannot be selected manually. See Chapter 7.

Channel 16 Over-Ride Fitted to most modern VHF sets, this facility selects Channel 16 instantly, enabling a 'working channel' to be pre-tuned prior to making the initial call on Channel 16 for the time being.

Channels M (157.85MHz) and M2 (161.425) These are additional, private channels for communication with British yacht clubs. They are only available on sets

Channel Designators	Transmitting Frequencies		Intership	Port Operations		Coast Radio Stations
	Ship Stations	Coast Stations		Simplex	Duplex	
60	156.025	160.625			2	1
01	156.050	160.650			1	
61	156.075	160.675				1
02	156.100	160.700				1
62	156.125	160.725				1
03	156.150	160.750				1
63	156.175	160.775				1
04	156.200	160.800				1
64	156.225	160.825				1
05	156.250	160.850				1
65	156.275	160.875				1
06	156.300		1			
66	156.325	160.925				1
07	156.350	160.950				1
67	156.375	156.375 — HM Coastguard — Small Ships Rescue Channel				
08	156.400		1			
68	156.425	156.425		1		
09	156.450	156.450	●			
69	156.475	156.475	●	●		
10	156.500	156.500 — Oil Pollution Channel				
70	**156.525**	**156.525 — Digital Selective Calling for Distress, Safety & Calling**				
11	156.550	156.550		1		
71	156.575	156.575		1		
12	156.600	156.600		1		
72	156.625	156.625	1			
13	156.650	156.650	●			
73	156.675	156.675 — HM Coastguard — Back-up Channel				
14	156.700	156.700		1		
74	156.725	156.725		1		
15	156.750	156.750	2	2		
75	GUARDBAND	THIS CHANNEL MAY NOT BE USED				
16	**156.800**	**156.800 — DISTRESS, SAFETY & CALLING**				
76	GUARDBAND	THIS CHANNEL MAY NOT BE USED				
17	156.850	156.850	2	2		
77	156.875		1			
18	156.900	161.500			1	
78	156.925	161.525			1	
19	156.950	161.550			1	
79	156.975	161.575			1	
20	157.000	161.600			1	
80	157.025	161.625			1	
21	157.050	161.650			1	
81	157.075	161.675				1
22	157.100	161.700			1	
82	157.125	161.725				1
23	157.150	161.750				1
83	157.175	161.775				1
24	157.200	161.800				1
84	157.225	161.825				1
25	157.250	161.850				1
85	157.275	161.875				1
26	157.300	161.900				1
86	157.325	161.925				1
27	157.350	161.950				1
87	157.375	161.975				1
28	157.400	162.000				1
88	157.425	162.025				1

Key to Table 6.1:
1 = Primary Use
2 = Secondary Use
● = Services have equal status

A marina lock-keeper using VHF to control boat movement on Ch 80 and Ch 'M'

sold in UK and only British yachts will be licensed to use them.

Wx Channels These are special channels fitted to sets sold in North America for receiving taped US and Canadian local weather reports on 10 private channels.

USA Channels In addition to the 55 international channels, the USA also uses some two-frequency port operations channels on a single frequency basis with the shore station (coastguard or port) transmitting on the ship's frequency. These are: 7A, 18A, 19A. 21A, 22A, 23A, 65A, 66A, 78A, 79A, 80A, 83A and 88A. All merchant ships in US waters are required to have sets with this facility and foreign yachts are strongly advised to do so. US coastguards broadcast on Channel 22A, while Canadian coastguards use it for ship–shore working.

Dual Watch and Scanning

Dual watch is a clever system which effectively enables the receiver section to monitor Channel 16 and any working channel simultaneously by alternately switching between the two. The set spends most of its time on the working channel but locks on to Channel 16 as soon as a signal is received. When a signal is received on the working channel, however, the set will continue to switch occasionally back to Channel 16 so reception will be interrupted briefly. It is a very useful facility which allows listening out for a friend on a pre-arranged working channel while, at the same time, maintaining listening watch on Ch.16. Under the GMDSS, Channel 13 is designated as a working channel for intership safety messages and many merchant ships voluntarily monitor Channels 13 and 16 in coastal waters. This would be good practice for small craft, too.

With the final implimentation of the GMDSS on 1. February 1999, Ch.16 is designated as being reserved exclusively for Distress traffic with routine calls and Distress Alerts being made by DSC on Channel 70. However, until all small craft are fitted with Digital Selective Calling (DSC), the tradition of making initial calls by voice on Channel 16 is being allowed to continue for the time being.

Some sets boast a scanning facility for automatically switching through many or all channels in turn. On receipt of a signal, the scanning stops temporarily.

NOTE: Dual Watch or scanning must be switched off before transmitting.

Squelch

The extremely high amplification of modern radios brings with it a very loud hissing sound when no signal is being received. This can be objectionable when listening out on Channel 16, for example. The squelch circuit effectively (though not actually) disconnects the loudspeaker in the absence of a signal but instantly reconnects it when a signal is received. Thus, the background hiss is cut out between signals. On VHF sets, the control is variable and for best results it should be set at the point where the hissing noise only just stops. If the control is advanced any further, the receiver becomes insensitive to weak signals.

Many modem SSB sets also feature a squelch control operated by an on/off switch.

Power Control

The maximum transmitted power output of a Marine VHF set is 25 watts but it must be able to reduce output power to 1 watt or less. This is done by means of a switch on the front panel which may be rotary, toggle or push button. For normal operation, one watt is quite sufficient; as the range is determined by the horizon, not power, no increase in range will be achieved by an increase in power which will only cause unnecessary interference to other stations some distance away. A secondary benefit of using low power is that it draws much less current from the battery: about 1 amp against 5 or 6 amps on full power. This could be important in a small sailboat or with a hand held set where battery power is very limited. The high power facility is provided to give an overriding 'louder voice' in case of distress and urgency situations. High power is also recommended for telephone calls via Coast Radio Stations who like to put a strong signal down the line.

By contrast, SSB sets can usually switch between three or more power levels. On MF, power is selected to give the minimum power to achieve satisfactory communication on the basis of, roughly, 0.75 miles per watt. On HF, full power is the norm for long range, because the average 150 watt R/T in a yacht is competing with merchant ships using the maximum power of 1.5 kilowatts.

Range

VHF range at sea is line of sight determined by the height of the transmitting and receiving aerials. When these heights are known, several rnethods can be used to determine the range:

1. Nautical tables (Nories, Burtons, etc.) or almanacs (Macmillans, etc.) can be consulted for the 'distance of the sea horizon', 'extreme range' or 'dipping distance' pages. Although these tables were intended for vision, they are equally applicable to radio, the height(s) of aerial(s) being substituted for 'height of eye' or 'height of light'. Due to the slightly greater refraction of radio waves, the figures thus obtained may be increased by 10%.

2. The range can be calculated from simple formulae:

a) Range in **statute** miles to the horizon = $\sqrt{2h}$ where h = height of aerial in feet. So aerial-to-aerial range = $\sqrt{2h}$ Tx + $\sqrt{2h}$ Rx.

b) Aerial-to-aerial range in **nautical** miles = $2.25\sqrt{h}$ Tx + $2.25\sqrt{h}$ Rx, where h = height of aerial in metres (Tx = transmitter; Rx = receiver).

7

The GMDSS (Global Maritime Distress and Safety System)

Finally implemented on 1 February 1999, the GMDSS utilizes MF/HF and VHF radios, communication satellites and EPIRBs. Until 1999, marine radio contact was first established by R/T on a designated *calling* frequency/channel before changing to a *working* frequency/channel for the exchange of messages. Under the GMDSS, however, initial *Alerts* (Distress, Urgency, Safety and Routine) should now be made by new *digital* technology called **Digital Selective Calling (DSC)** on *new* DSC frequencies. This involves programming a mini computer screen on *new* GMDSS radios or DSC Controllers. Sadly, the old traditional VHF and SSB radios cannot be modified or upgraded to comply with GMDSS requirements. It must be emphasized that this new DSC system only applies to the initial call or **Alert** as it is termed in DSC-speak; **traditional voice message procedures follow and are unchanged**.

Although the GMDSS is not mandatory for small craft under 300 gross tonnage (gt), it is prudent to do so voluntarily. Mandatory watch on 2182kHz and Channel 16 officially ceased in 1999 but, as leisure craft vastly outnumber commercial craft, they and Coastguards will keep voluntary watch on Channel 16 for the time being.

THE GENERAL PLAN

Under the GMDSS, all the World's navigable water is divided into four Sea Areas:

Sea Area A1

Sea Area A1 is defined as 'within radiotelephone coverage of at least one VHF coast station in which continuous alerting by Digital Selective Calling (DSC) is available'. As the range of VHF is determined almost entirely by the height of the respective aerials, no general range can be given. A specific range is published for each station depending on the height of its aerial. For example, The Netherlands quotes 18 miles for all their stations but several stations in Greece and Turkey quote over 100 miles! The average is about 35 miles.

The ICOM IC–M802 MF/HF Marine Transceiver

Sea Area A2

Sea Area A2, briefly, is within MF R/T range of the shore (but excluding Sea Area A1). As the range of MF (by day) is determined by the transmitted power, no general figure can be given. The UK has declared an MF range of 150 miles for all stations (the average for most stations) but other stations have declared ranges between 60 miles (Japan) and 500 miles (Mexico).

Sea Area A3

Sea Area A3 is defined as 'within coverage of an INMARSAT geostationary satellite but excluding Sea Areas A1 and A2' (i.e., oceanic areas).

Sea Area A4

Sea Area A4 is defined as 'outside Sea Areas 1, 2 & 3'. In practice, this means Polar Regions as the INMARSAT satellite coverage does not extend above 70° North or 70° South.

For a full explanation of the GMDSS and a directory of all participating shore stations, see ALRS, Vol. 5.

CARRIAGE REQUIREMENTS

Since 1 February 1999, all ships over 300gt sailing on international voyages within Sea Area A1 have been required to carry a DSC VHF set with Channel 70 watchkeeping facilities *plus* a NAVTEX receiver *plus* a 406MHz EPIRB *plus* one or more *waterproof* hand-held VHF sets for on-scene rescue operations.

For sailing within Sea Area A2, the same ship must also carry MF/SSB equipment with DSC and 2187.5kHz watchkeeping facilities *in addition* to all the equipment for an A1 area.

For oceanic voyages in Sea Area A3, ships have the option of carrying GMDSS-approved INMARSAT satellite equipment or HF/SSB equipment with DSC facilities and a DSC watchkeeping receiver for 8414.5kHz and at least one of the other four new HF Distress Alerting frequencies (usually, a scanning receiver is fitted which continuously scans all six MF/HF DSC Distress frequencies) *plus* all the equipment required for Sea Areas A1 and A2.

For those ships brave (or foolish) enough to venture into Sea Area A4 above 70° N or S, GMDSS-approved HF/SSB sets are mandatory as the ship will be beyond INMARSAT coverage.

In Sea Areas A3 and A4, 100% duplication of equipment is required if a qualified Radio-Electronics Officer (a new post) is not carried.

NEW IDENTIFICATION

For DSC purposes, a new system of identifying GMDSS radio stations has been introduced. As well as a station or ship's name and call-sign, GMDSS radio stations now have a nine-digit 'telephone' number called a Maritime Mobile Service Identity (MMSI). This is freely issued by the Radio Regulatory Authority at the time the vessel is first licensed or at its annual renewal. Like a telephone number, the first three figures, called Maritime Identification Digits (MID), are the 'country code'. For example, all UK MMSIs start with 232, 233, 234 or 235 in the same way that all UK callsigns start with 'G', 'M' or '2'. All mainland USA MMSIs start with 366, 367 or 368 (Alaska, 303; Hawaii, 338) just as USA callsigns start with 'K', 'N' or 'W'. The remaining six digits identify the ship uniquely. Ship and shore-station names, callsigns and MMSIs are listed in the ITU *List of Call Signs & Numerical Identities* from chandlers and nautical bookshops and also from the following website 'www.itu.int/itu-r/terrestrial/mars/index.html'.

The authorized MMSI is entered into new small-craft Class D VHF sets by the first owner *but only one attempt is allowed.* For transfer to another boat, the set must first be returned to the manufacturer for neutralization. In addition to this unique MMSI, however, an authorized temporary 'Group' MMSI, distinguished by a 'leading zero', can be self-programmed. For example, a race fleet or rally could have a common MMSI of 023200345. Shore stations are distinguished by two leading zeros. For example, Falmouth Coastguard is 002320014.

DISTRESS ALERTS

This is the new name given to the DSC-equivalent of the traditional R/T Distress *Call.*

However, in addition to the vessel's identification (built-in), the Distress *Alert* also gives the vessel's position (Latitude & Longitude), nature of distress and the channel or frequency for subsequent voice (or Telex) communication. Thus, **all the information necessary to initiate a Search and Rescue operation can be broadcast by anyone on board simply lifting a flap and pressing a big red button.** To improve reliability, the Distress Alert is automatically transmitted five times *and subsequently repeated every four minutes* until acknowledged or the vessel sinks. On VHF (Channel 70), the whole transmission takes about 1.5 seconds. On MF and HF, the transmission lasts nearly 1 minute. On HF, the Distress Alert can be sent five times on one frequency or once on each of the six new MF/HF distress frequencies of 2187.5, 4207.5, 6312, 8414.5, 12,557 and 16,804.5kHz. (This is not recommended except in desperate circumstances.) Refer to Table 7.1.

To reduce the possibility of sending false Distress Alerts accidentally, pressing the big red button marked 'DISTRESS' or 'SOS' does not, initially, send a Distress Alert; it merely displays four lines of information on a small screen. (All four lines may be displayed together or each line may have to be scrolled sequentially depending on the type of equipment.)

● The first line shows the transmit frequency. On VHF sets, this is Channel 70 and cannot be changed. On MF/HF/VHF (Class A) controllers, the frequency can be changed to one of the other six MF/HF frequencies shown in Table 7.1.
● The second line shows the 'nature of distress'. By default, this is always 'undesignated' (i.e., unspecified) but, if time allows, one of ten distress situations *which now includes Piracy Attack* and *Man Overboard* is quickly selected.
● The third line gives the vessel's position. By default, this shows 'no position specified' but, in this case, there is no point in sending a Distress Alert! The DSC

Table 7.1 – Radio Distress Communications			
	Digital Selective Calling (DSC)	Radiotelephone	Radiotelex
VHF	Channel 70	Channel 16	–
MF	2187.5kHz	2182.0kHz	2174.5kHz
HF4	4207.5kHz	4125.0kHz	4177.5kHz
HF6	6312.0kHz	6215.0kHz	6268.0kHz
HF8	8414.5kHz	8291.0kHz	8376.5kHz
HF12	12577.0kHz	12290.0kHz	12520.0kHz
HF16	16804.5kHz	16420.0kHz	16695.0kHz

controller or new VHF set can be interfaced with a GPS receiver which continuously updates the position and time. In the absence of a GPS receiver, the ship's position *and the current time (UTC/GMT)* must be entered manually by means of the numerical key-pad on the equipment. In this case, GMDSS Regulations demand that the position and *the time that the position was entered* be updated *at least every four hours* (i.e., once per watch).

● The last line ('Telecommand'), gives the mode of subsequent communication. On VHF, this is always 'Simplex Telephone' on Channel 16. On MF/HF, however, there is a simple choice of 'J3E' (voice) or Telex on the paired frequency. *For every one of the seven new Distress Alerting frequencies, there are paired voice and Telex communications frequencies in the same band* (see Table 7.1).

Once the Distress Alert has been composed, the red button must be pressed a second time *and held depressed for at least 5 seconds* to transmit the Alert.

The DSC Distress Alert should be immediately followed by the traditional 'MAYDAY' broadcast on the paired communications frequency/channel.

On receipt of a DSC Alert, an alarm sounds on all DSC-equipped ships and at coast stations called Maritime Rescue Co-ordination Centres (MRCCs) within range. (These are Coastguard Stations on VHF but could be Coast Radio Stations on MF and HF.) Alerted by the alarm, an MRCC officer prints out the details on the receiver's screen and immediately activates a DSC Distress Acknowledgement. S/he then switches to the paired R/T frequency/channel for the reception of the traditional voice 'Mayday'. The Search and Rescue operation is then initiated.

False Distress Alerts

In the unlikely event of a false Distress Alert being sent inadvertently, the following procedure should be adopted:

1. Allow the Alert to be completed.
2. Stop further repetitions by switching the equipment off or pressing the 'CANCEL' button.
3. Switch to the paired R/T frequency/channel and broadcast a cancellation by saying:
   'MAYDAY (once only)
   All Stations, All Stations, All Stations.
   This is MMSI, CALLSIGN, SHIP'S NAME.
   In position... (Lat & Long)
   Cancel my Distress Alert of DATE & TIME (UTC)
   Signed MASTER, MMSI, CALLSIGN, SHIP'S NAME.
   DATE & TIME (UTC)'

Other Alerts and Calls

As well as a big Red Button for DSC

DISTRESS, **U**rgency and **S**afety (DUS) Alerts, there may also be means of selecting 'DISTRESS ACKNOWLEDGE', 'DISTRESS RELAY', 'INDIVIDUAL', 'ACKNOWLEDGE', 'GROUP', 'GEOGRAPHIC AREA', 'TELEPHONE' and 'TEST CALL' options by DSC.

Note:
1. Not all these options are available on Class 'D' VHF or Class 'E' SSB sets.
2. DSC TEST CALLS should be made weekly to an MRCC on 2187.5kHz or HF.
3. Ch. 70 is used for *all* DSC Alerts: DUS and Individual. Voice 'radio checks' should be made with a nearby yacht, marina or harbour **on a working channel**.
4. Some new portable VHF sets can be allocated the distinctive MMSI prefix of 2359 for DSC Distress Alerts in UK waters **but they may not be able to send supporting information** such as position, type of Distress and so on.
5. On MF, 2187.5kHz is only used for DSC Alerts and Test Calls.
   Individual DSC Alerts **to** Coast Stations by MMSI are sent on 2189.5kHz with the acknowledgement received by the ship on 2177kHz.
   Individual DSC Alerts **from** Coast Stations are received on 2177kHz.
   Individual ship-to-ship DSC Calls by MMSI are sent on 2177kHz *and the acknowledgement also received on*

2177kHz.
6. On HF, *individual* ship-to-ship DSC Calls may be sent *and acknowledge*d on 4209, 6313, 8416, 12,578, 16,806, 18,899, 22,375 and 25,209kHz.
   NB, *For these*, the receive frequency must be programmed into the scanner in place of, say, the highest Distress Alert frequency of 16,804.5kHz.
7. Having made contact by DSC, *voice* communication then takes place on the frequency or channel indicated by the station called.

ACKNOWLEDGEMENTS

DSC Distress, Urgency and Safety Alerts and Individual Calls (to other ships or the shore) and Test Calls *(on MF or HF only)* to MRCCs will be acknowledged by DSC. *A DSC Distress Acknowledgement automatically stops any further repetitions of the Alert **and puts the acknowledging station in control of the situation. Therefore, ships do not, normally, acknowledge a DSC Distress Alert by DSC***.

In Sea Area A1 it can be assumed that a VHF DSC Distress Alert will have been received by an MRCC/MRSC which will acknowledge and take control. The correct procedure for other ships is to record the details on the DSC screen, then set watch on Channel 16 and listen for the subsequent traditional 'Mayday' broadcast. If there is no reply from the shore within three minutes, the 'Mayday' should be acknowledged *by voice* on Channel 16 and an MRCC/ MRSC advised.

In Sea Area A2, MF procedure is similar except that the 'Mayday' could be preceded by the two-tone alarm (if possible) and the frequency will be 2182kHz.

In Sea Areas A3 and A4, HF procedure is also similar except that watch should be set on the paired R/T frequency (see Table 7.1). If no reply has been heard *after five minutes*, a 'Distress/Mayday Relay' should be addressed to an MRCC *by any means* (DSC, voice, Telex or satellite).

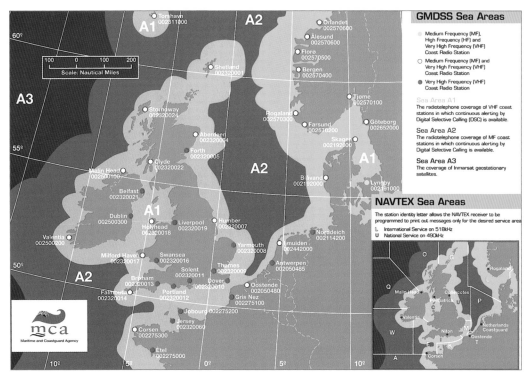

Figure 7.1   GMDSS Sea Areas courtesy of The Navigation and Communications Branch, The Maritime and Coastguard Agency, Spring Place, 105 Commercial Road, Southampton, SO15 1EG, UK

*   Exceptionally, ships may acknowledge DSC Distress Alerts by DSC when it is quite certain that the Alert has not been received by a MRCC/MRSC. There are two classic examples:

a.   If a *repeated* DSC Distress Alert is received every four minutes; or

b.   If a DSC Distress Alert is sent *in an inappropriate Sea Area*, e.g., on Channel 70 outside Sea Area A1 or on 2187.5kHz outside Sea Area A2.

In these unlikely circumstances, nearby vessels should send a DSC Distress Acknowledgement, and if possible, then advise an MRCC/MRSC *by any means*.

NB – On the new small-craft Class D VHF and Class E SSB sets, DSC Distress Relays *and* DSC Distress Acknowledgements cannot be sent.

8

Distress, Urgency and Safety

PRIORITY OF SIGNALS

Priority 1: Distress Signal

Top priority is given to Distress Signals which have absolute precedence over all other communications. Distress calls are prefixed by the word 'Mayday' (French 'm'aidez' - 'come to my aid') spoken three times to indicate that a *vessel* is in grave and imminent danger (e.g. sinking or on fire) and requests immediate assistance. In other words, a catastrophic disaster is about to overtake the whole vessel. So 'Mayday' does not apply to 'man overboard' or personal injuries (but see Chapt. 7). Following a DSC Distress Alert on an appropriate frequency (if possible), the initial Distress Message is broadcast (i.e. not addressed) by voice on the Distress frequencies of 2182, 4125, 6215, 8291, 12290, 16420kHz, Ch. 16 or any other frequency authorized by the Master. All subsequent Distress messages are prefixed by 'Mayday' once only and sent on these same frequencies. During a Distress situation, radio silence is imposed until cancelled by the controlling station broadcasting the phrase 'Seelonce Feenee' (French 'Silence Finis').

Initially, the distressed vessel is in control since it is the first to know! On receipt of the

DSC Distress Alert and subsequent Distress Message ashore, control will be assumed by a Maritime Rescue Co-ordination Centre (MRCC) or Maritime Rescue Sub-Centre (MRSC). In Sea Areas A1 and A2, these will be Coastguard Stations on MF/VHF. Offshore, the MRCC could be a traditional HF Coast Radio Station. If no acknowledgement is heard from the shore after 3-5 minutes, vessels in the area should send a DSC Distress Relay or Mayday Relay.

Priority 2: Urgency Signal

Following a DSC 'All Ships Urgency' Alert, all other emergencies are indicated by the prefix 'Pan-Pan' (French 'panne' - 'in difficulty') also spoken 3 times on the Distress frequencies. This is not a cry for help but a plea for priority which comes a very close second to 'Mayday'. It indicates that the station has a very urgent message to send concerning the safety of a ship *or a person* (e.g. serious injuries or man overboard). Pan-Pan is not a broadcast so the call must be addressed to a particular station e.g. a Coastguard or 'All Stations'. The initial call and short message is sent on a Distress frequency but long or medical messages will be transferred to a working frequency. Like Distress, radio silence is automatically imposed during the exchange of messages but normal working may be resumed if nothing is heard for three minutes. There is no advice of end of radio silence.

Priority 3: Safety Signals

Messages concerning safety of navigation are announced initially on 2182kHz and/or Channel 16 by the prefix 'Sécurité' (say-cure-ee-tay; safety) three times following a DSC 'ALL Ships Safety' Alert. The call must include the working frequency of the subsequent message. It is usually used by shore stations for broadcasts of navigational warnings, gale warnings, etc. but, exceptionally, may be used to broadcast to 'all ships' by a vessel beyond VHF range of the shore, for example, a yacht becalmed in the busy shipping lane half-way across the Bay of Biscay. After a DSC 'All Ships Safety' alert or initial call on Channel 16, the message would be broadcast on Channel 13, the intership safety channel. Radio silence is imposed during transmission but ends with the end of the broadcast.

DISTRESS PROCEDURE

As Distress signals are broadcast for reception by people of all nationalities, a prescribed sequence must be followed to ensure rescue - and pass the exam!

Following a DSC Distress Alert on a suitable DSC frequency, the Distress Call and Message are broadcast on the associated Distress voice frequency.

1. The Distress Call to alert the World and impose radio silence:

"MAYDAY, MAYDAY, MAYDAY;
THIS IS (MMSI and callsign, callsign, callsign)".

2. The Distress Message immediately follows with all necessary information.

"MAYDAY (once again)

THIS IS MMSI, callsign (once again) and NAME (of vessel) ;

MY POSITION IS (Lat. & Long. or range & bearing *from* a reference point);

NATURE OF DISTRESS (e.g. sinking, on fire, etc.);

ASSISTANCE REQUIRED

ANY FURTHER INFORMATION; OVER"

Small craft sinking or on fire simply "Request immediate assistance" but, if disabled and drifting towards rocks, "Request immediate tow".

FURTHER INFORMATION should first state the number of people on board. Just count heads - including the Skipper! If there is time, state the colour, type and size of yacht plus any action being taken such as abandoning to liferaft, preparing flares or Personal Locator Beacon (PLB) on hearing aircraft, etc. "OVER" is always the last word, even before abandonment.

Obviously, the distress procedure is of vital importance to every sailor from the aspect of personal safety but, also, to pass the operational exam. The prescribed sequence of the distress message is easily remembered by the mnemonic 'MIPDANIO':

M	**M**ayday
I	**I**dentity
P	**P**osition
D	Nature of **D**istress
A	**A**ssistance required
N	**N**umber of people on board
I	Any other **I**nformation
O	**O**ver

Remember: This is the key to the Distress Message which follows the Distress Call. Example: Yacht 'Flash' (GRTO), has been holed by a semi-submerged container about 350 miles East of Barbados and is rapidly sinking. After sending a DSC Distress Alert on, say, 8414.5kHz (or all six MF/HF frequencies), the following would be broadcast *at full power* on 8291kHz.

"MAYDAY, MAYDAY, MAYDAY;

This is Two, Tree, Two; Six, Niner, Zero; Ait, Fife, Tree;
Golf, Romeo, Tango, Oscar;
Golf, Romeo, Tango, Oscar;
Golf, Romeo, Tango, Oscar;
MAYDAY;
Two Tree Two, Six Niner Zero, Ait Fife Tree;
Golf, Romeo, Tango, Oscar;
Yacht 'FLASH'

Position zero-niner-zero, Barbados, tree-fife-zero miles;

Slowly sinking; request immediate assistance;

Fower people on board; preparing to abandon to liferaft.

Sailing yacht 'FLASH'; I spell: Foxtrot, Lima, Alpha, Sierra, Hotel;

Ten metre sloop; white hull and sails; sail number: ait-six-two Yankee;

Will activate aircraft PLB on hearing aircraft;

OVER".

This DSC Distress Alert and subsequent voice message on HF would be received by CAMSLANT (USCG Communications Area Master Station Atlantic) which would immediately initiate a Search And Rescue (SAR) operation. Without a DSC facility, there is little chance that a 'Mayday' on 2182kHz (even during the obsolete Silence Period) would be heard by other vessels in the area. A 'Mayday' on 8764kHz may be heard by Barbados Radio who could pass the details on to the USCG Station at Miami but this cannot be guaranteed.

This illustrates the tremendous advantage of DSC. All the essential details can be broadcast worldwide in one minute, giving more time for abandonment.

Acknowledgement of Distress Message

On hearing a Distress Message:

1. Listen and note the date, time and content of the message on the notepad with the pencil which is alongside the radio – isn't it?

2. Wait three minutes (five minutes on HF) to ensure that the Distress Alert is not acknowledged by an MRCC. If it is, keep quiet unless you can offer help.

If it is not acknowledged:
3. *Do not acknowledge by DSC.*
Acknowledge on voice frequency, saying:

"MAYDAY (name or callsign of distressed vessel three times);

This is (your own ship's name or callsign three times);

RECEIVED MAYDAY, OVER."

If you are able to offer practical assistance, add this information to your acknowledgement.

4. Tell the World on HF, 2182kHz or Channel 16 by saying:

"Mayday Relay, Mayday Relay, Mayday Relay;

This is (identity, identity, identity);

The following message was received from (distressed vessel) at (time);

Message begins…

The Operations Room, Solent MRSC, Lee-on-Solent, UK. The Operators are from left to right: Channel 'O' Desk, Watch Manager, Channel 67/73 Desk & Channel 16 Desk

Message ends;

Over."

If you hear a Distress Message acknowledged by an MRCC/MRSC and are able to offer assistance, call them by preceding their name with the word 'Mayday'. (All messages concerning Distress are prefixed by the word 'Mayday'.)

If you hear the Distress Alert and Message acknowledged by an MRCC/MRSC and are not able to offer assistance, *keep quiet!*

On seeing a Distress Signal

Send a DSC Distress Relay if possible (not on Class D or E sets) then broadcast the information on an appropriate Distress voice frequency by saying:

"Mayday Relay, Mayday Relay, Mayday Relay;

This is (your own ship's name or callsign three times);

My position is (Lat. and Long. or range & bearing *from* a reference point)

Type of Distress Signal seen,

Time Distress Signal was seen,

Position of Distress Signal seen or range and bearing *from* your own position.

Over".

TWO-TONE ALARM

Up to 23.59, UTC (GMT) on 31 January 1999, all Coastguards, Coast Radio Stations, cargo ships over 300 tons and passenger vessels on international voyages were required to carry a dedicated 2182kHz 'watchkeeping receiver'. The loudspeaker was normally muted but became 'live' on receiving a distinctive police car-type warbling siren generated within marine SSB transmitters. In cases of Distress and *Man Overboard* (MOB), the alarm was sent immediately prior to broadcasting the Distress (or Pan-Pan) Call and Message. This activated hundreds of loudspeakers within a 200-mile radius enabling all mariners, ashore and afloat, to hear the alarm and the voice signal following. The alarm lasted about 45 seconds – usually timed automatically.

Although no longer mandatory, it is worth remembering that many older ships and Coastguard Stations still retain these watchkeeping receivers. Before broadcasting a Mayday or Pan-Pan for MOB, it would be prudent to send the alarm first. It is still fitted to many GMDSS SSB transceivers. Several schemes prevented accidental transmission – either a 'Test Alarm' button and a red 'Alarm' button simultaneously or the red 'Alarm' button and the PTT switch or pressing the 'Alarm' button for 2+ seconds. Pressing the 'Alarm' button quickly or pressing the 'Test Alarm' button alone enabled the alarm tones (1300Hz and 2200Hz) to be heard in the set's loudspeaker or handset earpiece. Sending the Alarm often switched the transceiver to H3E on 2182kHz automatically.

URGENCY PROCEDURE

Calls concerning the safety of a vessel *or person* such as dismasting, engine failure, lack of fuel, steering problems, man-overboard, diving accidents, etc., should be addressed to a Coastguard by prefixing what would otherwise have been a routine call by the phrase 'Pan-Pan' three times. *Brief* details of the problem can be included in the initial call on 2182kHz or Channel 16 to enable nearby ships to ascertain whether or not they could help. (NB, Non-Distress transmissions must not exceed one minute on designated Distress frequencies.)

EXAMPLE: The yacht 'Flash', call-sign GRTO, has been dismasted about 80 miles East of Cape Cod. Following a DSC 'All Ships Urgency' on 2187.5kHz, the following voice message would be transmitted *with full power* on 2182kHz:

"Pan-Pan, Pan-Pan, Pan-Pan;

Boston Coastguard, Boston Coastguard, Boston Coastguard;

This is Two Tree Two, Six Niner Zero, Fife Ait Tree;
Golf, Romeo, Tango, Oscar;
Golf, Romeo, Tango, Oscar;
Golf, Romeo, Tango, Oscar;

British yacht 'Flash'; I spell: Foxtrot, Lima, Alpha, Sierra, Hotel;

My position fower-one, fife-ait North; six-fife, fife-zero West;

Dismasted and bound Provincetown under power;

Fower people on board; making tree knots in heavy seas;

Request safety services stand-by, please.

OVER."

This call would be acknowledged by Boston Coastguard who would probably transfer Flash to a working frequency for further information.

QUESTION: If the skipper of *Flash* has lost his mast, *he has also lost his backstay aerial!* So, how did he manage to talk to Boston Coastguard on MF? As a prudent yachtsman, of course, he would not dream of going to sea without emergency aerials! A small one for VHF which could be quickly stuck on top of a deck-brush handle and lashed to a guardrail and a 7m/23ft. sectional MF whip which would be fitted into a mounting already fixed to the after-deck.

Any search-and-rescue (SAR) aircraft looking for Flash would be able to communicate with him on 2182kHz, MF, and Channels 16 and 6, VHF.

MEDICAL ADVICE OR ASSISTANCE

Specific instructions for obtaining medical

advice or assistance from any maritime country are in a section at the back of ALRS, Volume 1. Every European state provides one or more Radio Medical Advice Centres who are usually contacted via an MRCC/MRSC. They can freely connect you to a specialist doctor or the International Radio Medical Centre (CIRM) in Italy (who speak English). In addition to the symptoms, the doctor will also need details of the patient such as age, sex, ethnic origin, etc., *and the contents of the Ship's Medicine Chest* so these details should be readily available. He may refer to the *Ship Captains' Medical Guide* or the (better) *W.H.O. International Medical Guide For Ships.* The blue pages at the back of the *IMO International Code of Signals* show the 'naming of parts', over 300 symptoms, 94 common diseases and 38 common medicines. If the doctor decides that medical *assistance* is required and you are within range of a helicopter, he can arrange for a CASEVAC. Otherwise the MRCC would try to contact a doctor-equipped ship in the area. Ideally, a DSC 'Individual Urgency' or 'All Ships Urgency' Alert is made on a distress frequency followed by a 'Pan-Pan' call by voice on the associated speech frequency to the station who replies.

INMARSAT is easier; code 32 gets medical *advice*, code 38 gets medical *assistance* and code 39 brings *maritime* assistance (pumps, tows, etc).

When well offshore, remember that many large merchant ships and all large warships carry doctors and a small sick-bay. Large cruise ships are especially well equipped with highly-skilled doctors and well-fitted hospitals. A DSC 'All Ships Urgency' Alert and a *'Pan-Pan'* call (3 times) to "All Ships" or "Any (War)ship" on Channel 16 and/or 2182kHz should elicit a reply.

Safety Procedure

Safety signals are not, normally, the concern of a yacht except when receiving gale warnings, navigational warnings, etc.

However, there is still a valid case for yachts to transmit a Sécurité message when reporting a navigational hazard to a Coastguard or making an 'All Ships Safety' *broadcast* when offshore.

EXAMPLE: Yacht *'Flash'* is becalmed half-way across the Bay of Biscay in the main shipping lane. Ideally, an 'All Ships Safety' Alert should first be made on 2187.5kHz and/or an initial announcement on 2182kHz would be:

"Sécurité, Sécurité, Sécurité;

All ships, all ships, all ships;

This is (MMSI); Golf, Romeo, Tango, Oscar; Golf, Romeo, Tango, Oscar;

For Navigational Warning, listen Two, Zero, Fower, Ait; Over."

The transmitter *and receiver* would then be tuned to 2048kHz and the following broadcast made after a short pause:

"Sécurité, Sécurité, Sécurité;

All ships, all ships, all ships.

This is (MMSI); Golf, Romeo, Tango, Oscar; Golf, Romeo, Tango, Oscar;

British yacht *'Flash'*, I spell: Foxtrot, Lima, Alpha, Sierra, Hotel;

Position: four-six, zero-one North; zero-seven, two-ait West;

Sailing Yacht *'Flash'* becalmed and not under command (NUC);

Vessels advised keep sharp look-out and give wide berth;

This is *'Flash'* OUT."

If the NUC situation is likely to last several hours, the French Coastguard Service, C.R.O.S.S. (Centres Regionaux Operationnels de Surveillance et de Sauvetage) at Étel near

McMurdo's Fastfind Plus Personal Location Beacon (above) and the Precision 406 MHz GPS EPIRB (right) both have integral GPS for pin-point location of 30 metres compared to 3 nm for the first generation EPIRBs

Lorient could be advised and asked to include the information on their sceduled navigation warning broadcasts. They are responsible for marine safety throughout the whole of the Bay of Biscay.

The same broadcast could also be made on Channel 13, VHF following a DSC 'All Ships Safety' Alert on Channel 70 but this would have to be repeated every 30 minutes

due to the short ship-to-ship range of VHF.

In the meantime *Flash* would display appropriate day and night NUC signals.

EPIRBs and SARTs

Both of these are non-communication devices to signal Distress and indicate the position of a distressed vessel and/or survivors in the water or liferaft. EPIRBs operate through one of two satellite systems; SARTs produce a distinctive picture on the 3cm radar of a nearby ship or SAR aircraft.

EPIRBs

The first Emergency Position-Indicating Radio Beacons transmitted an alarm signal on 2182kHz but were soon superseded by much smaller types which transmitted a swept-tone alarm on the two *aircraft* Distress frequencies of 121.5MHz (civil) and 243MHz (military). Aviators call them Emergency Location Transmitters (ELTs); mountaineers call them Personal Locator Beacons (PLBs). *They are not intended as Distress beacons at sea.* Aeronautical land stations would not hear a yacht at sea and civil aircraft do not, normally, maintain listening watch on 121.5MHz until well beyond Air Traffic Control range. Until recently, signals from these EPIRBs could also be picked up by dedicated COPAS-SARSAT satellites which could fix a *rough* position but their coverage was not World-wide. The satellite service on 121.5MHz is now discontinued.

In the GMDSS, the old 121.5MHz EPIRBs have been superseded by dedicated marine EPIRBs which operate, principally, on 406MHz. Activation can be manual or automatic upon immersion; they float and a few metres of line are carried for attachment to the liferaft. A 121.5MHz signal is also incorporated but this is purely for 'homing' or pin-point location. Identification is by 15-digit ID number which must be registered with your national EPIRB Registry (Falmouth Coastguard for UK vessels). The registration

Working wrist watch & Man Overboard Beacon

form supplied with new EPIRBs (and UK Ship Radio Licence Guidance Notes) also requires other details such as name, callsign, MMSI and type of vessel, maximum number of people carried, name and address of owner and telephone number of a shore contact.

The first generation of COSPAS-SARSAT satellites consists of four satellites in Low Earth Orbit (LEO-SAR) around the Poles. Thus, the Earth revolves inside a four-bar 'cage' so that, *eventually*, the whole World is covered. Location of older-type EPIRBs is done by Doppler Shift which could take up to two hours before an MRCC is advised and a search initiated!

This problem has recently been resolved by the launching of three SAR (Search And Rescue) *geostationary* satellites, GEO-SAR, and the latest EPIRBs which incorporate a GPS receiver. GEO-SAR cannot cover Polar regions but between 70° N and 70° S, the EPIRB's GPS position is soon passed to an MRCC.

The solution to every skipper's MOB nightmare is a small, waterproof canister EPIRB or wristwatch PLB worn by each crew-member. When activated, manually or automatically upon immersion, the canister

transmits on 406MHz and 121.5MHz; the wristwatch on 121.5MHz only. Both sound an alarm at an on-board receiver which indicates the direction of the casualty.

INMARSAT EPIRBs

The newest EPIRBs send a Distress signal to one of the four INMARSAT geostationary *communication* satellites on a frequency of around 1.6GHz and are alternatively known as INMARSAT-E, L-Band EPIRBs or 1.6GHz EPIRBs. Like the GEO-SAR satellites, they only cover latitudes between 70° North and 70° South but this will satisfy most sensible sailors! They also carry the 121.5MHz homing signal which can be picked up by direction-finding (D/F or RDF) receivers on SAR lifeboats and aircraft, some passenger vessels and oil rig standby vessels.

Some INMARSAT EPIRBs can be remotely programmed with 'type of Distress' information; some can be programmed on the housing for carriage into a liferaft and others incorporate a SART.

Other types

The GMDSS Regulations allow for the provision of VHF Channel 70 EPIRBs but it is believed that, as yet, only one is available (2003).

NOTES:

a) Float-free housings are not recommended for EPIRBs in small craft. Take an EPIRB, SART *and a hand-held VHF* in the 'panic bag' into the liferaft.

b) EPIRBs must be switched on *then secured to the liferaft and placed in the water* where they will float close by. *They must not be used inside the raft* as the aluminized canopy shields the signal and white strobe light on top.

c) They should be tested monthly *using the test switch provided* (read the instructions). The battery expiry date should also be checked at this time.

d) For carriage to and from the boat, the battery should be removed to prevent accidental activation. If this is not possible, aluminium kitchen foil should be doubly-wrapped around the aerial to shield accidental radiation.

e) In case of accidental activation, the nearest MRCC/MRSC should be informed immediately, **before switching off**. The MRCC/MRSC will then advise.

SART (Search and Rescue (Radar) Transponder)

These devices, about the size of 406MHz EPIRBs (12"/300mm), are developed from IFF (Identification, Friend or Foe) invented during WW2 to distinguish British radar-guided fighter aircraft from those of the enemy at night. This development is now used in all commercial (and some private) aircraft.

SART rigged on a survival craft

SARTs are the main means of locating distressed vessels and/or their survivors. They should be deployed at least 1m above sea level (for which an integral mast is often supplied) and *outside* the liferaft unless a special plastic housing is incorporated into the canopy. At the minimum height of 1m, their range is 5–10 miles to merchant ships and 40 miles to an SAR aircraft flying at 3,000ft.

The top section houses a 9GHZ (3cm) transceiver. When activated, the receiver section is empowered but the transmitter section remains inactive. Upon receiving a standard 3cm radar signal from a nearby ship or aircraft, the transmitter is triggered to return a distinctive, enhanced 'echo'.

At maximum range, the returned signal paints a line of 12 dots on the radar screen set to its 12-mile (later, 6-mile) range. The innermost dot is at the SART's position; the other 11 dots form a line towards the bearing scale. With the radar set to head-up display, the ship or aircraft has only to steer along the line of dots towards the SART. At about one mile from the SART, the outer end of the

dotted line begins to open out to form a fan shape. (At this point, ships should be slowing to avoid over-running the survivors!) As the range closes, the 'fan' progressively widens to form 12 concentric circles centred on the screen. The ship should now be stopped as the SART is beneath its bow!

In its 'idling' condition, the SART displays a white light which flashes once every two seconds. When its transmitter is triggered by a radar signal, the light becomes steady and an internal 'beep' sounds. Very reassuring to survivors!

Note:
a) **A SART must not be used in conjunction with a radar reflector**; this could obscure the SART from incoming signals.
b) SARTs should also be tested monthly by using the test key provided. Hold the SART several metres from your own radar and observe the 12 circles on the screen. **Do not look closely at the radar scanner – danger of eye damage!** The SART should be showing a steady light and 'beeping'.

Testing should be carried out as quickly as possible to avoid alerting nearby ships. Even in port, many vessels keep their 3cm radar running. Before replacing the SART in its cradle, check the battery's expiry date.

c) When 'idling', the battery should last 96 hours (4 days) and 8 hours once the transmitter has been triggered. This raises an important point. The SART should be left inactive until there is a good chance that it will be triggered by a ship or SAR aircraft *in sight*. If a SART is activated with the yacht abandoned on a deserted sea, the battery could expire before a ship or SAR aircraft appears. The SART illustrated is activated by inserting a finger through a film seal to reach a push switch but *it can only be switched off by inserting the testing key into a small hole in the back of the housing*! Therefore, it would be prudent to take the key into the liferaft so that the SART may be switched off if it fails to attract a passing ship. This saves the battery for further attempts.

d) Full details of the GMDSS, EPIRBs and SARTs are to be found in ALRS, Vol. 5.

9

Routine Procedure

Before pressing the 'Call' button or PTT switch, give some thought to several important questions:

- Does the call have priority?
- What is the purpose of the call?
- On what frequency or channel is the call to be made?
- Is the frequency or channel clear of other traffic?
- How is the other station addressed?
- Is the call authorised by the Master?
- How do I ensure that the call will be understood?

While priority may seem the first consideration, there is no point in making the call unless you are confident of being understood so at this stage you should make yourself fluent with the Phonetic Alphabet in Chapter 13 and the procedural words (PROWORDS) in the Appendix.

PRIORITIES

1. Distress

Distress signals take precedence over all others. Under GMDSS, the initial routine call should be made by DSC but if this is not available on small craft, a traditional voice call on Channel 16 or 2182kHz is the only alternative. Before calling on Channel 16 or 2182kHz, first listen for at least three minutes

to ensure that no distress, urgency or safety situation is extant. As stated in Chapter 8, radio silence is automatically imposed during a distress situation until ended by the controlling station broadcasting the phrase '**Seelonce Feenee**' (French 'silence finis' meaning end of radio silence) on the Distress frequency in use. Should radio silence be inadvertently broken, it will be imposed by the controlling station broadcasting the phrase, '**Seelonce Mayday**'.

2. Urgency

The *Urgency* call '**Pan-Pan**' (French panne) spoken three times, comes a close second in priority to distress and indicates that the calling station has a very urgent message to transmit concerning the safety of a vessel *or person. It is not necessarily a cry for help* but a demand for radio silence. Radio silence must be maintained throughout but normal working may be resumed three minutes after the last message. There is no announcement of cessation of silence.

3. Safety

This third priority concerns *navigational* safety and covers gale and navigation warnings, SAR relays, etc. It is indicated by the prefix **Sécurité** as in French (say-cure-ee-tay) three times. Usually used by Coast

Stations but may be used by ships out of range of the shore. Radio silence is imposed during transmission but normal working may be resumed immediately afterwards.

Other ships

Other ships may be called on matters of ship's business such as safety, medical advice, navigation, etc. In coastal waters, the VHF band should not be used for idle chit-chat. Only four VHF channels are reserved exclusively for ship-to-ship operation (6, 8, 72, 77) and they are shared by *all* vessels including the QM2! Ideally, individual ships should be called by DSC on Channel 70 but if this is unavailable, they can be called by voice directly on one of the four intership channels by prior arrangement. Otherwise by voice on Channel 16 after listening for at least three minutes to ensure that no priority signals are extant.

Likewise on MF, other ships should be called by DSC on 2177kHz or by voice directly on any intership frequency 2261-2498kHz, 3340-3397kHz and 3500-3596kHz *in 3kHz increments*. Suggestions such as 2300, 2333, 2345, 2468kHz, etc. are easily remembered. Otherwise by voice on 2182kHz after listening for at least three minutes. NOTE: For many decades before GMDSS, a mandatory three-minute Silence Period was imposed on 2182kHz from the hour and half-hour during which SOLAS vessels listened for distress traffic. Although no longer mandatory, ships are requested to still maintain this tradition voluntarily.

Some HF frequencies are available for intership DSC Routine Alerts. Otherwise, a 'sked' (schedule) can be arranged with the other vessel(s) to listen-out on one of the many intership frequencies in Table 9.1. Others are found in Section C of Appendix 16 to ALRS, Volume 1. Section A lists voice calling frequencies of *4125, 6215*, 8255, *12290, 16420*, 18795, 22060 and 25097kHz. **NOTE:** Frequencies in italics are also used for voice Distress, Urgency and Safety traffic.

NB: See pages 77 and 93 for GMDSS and useful frequencies.

Coastguards

They are addressed '(location) coastguard' and may be called *on matters of safety* concerning the vessel or anyone on board. All coastguards monitor Channel 16 VHF but some also monitor 2182 kHz for Distress signals. Around the British Isles (and Australia) all coastguards will then instruct a change to Channel 67 following a non-urgent call on Channel 16 VHF. US and Canadian coastguards work on Channel 22A (see Chapter 6) but others differ.

Port Authorities

Port or harbour authorities and pilots should be called for harbour advice or control. Most major ports are now run on similar lines to airports and require merchant ships to seek permission to enter, leave or manoeuvre within the port. In most cases, this mandatory requirement does not apply to pleasure vessels but at some (like Dover) it does. It is always best to ask; it does no harm, costs nothing and is common courtesy anyway. Likewise, small pleasure vessels are usually exempt from pilotage but it is worth checking.

Some ports or harbours *must* be called initially on Channel 16 VHF; some *may* be called on Channel 16 but an increasing number must be called directly on their working channel. Although most major ports maintain a 24 hour watch, many small harbours do not. They may work office hours, weekdays only, an hour or two either side of high water or when a vessel is expected. This information and much more, such as how the harbour/port is addressed and on what frequency or VHF channel, is detailed in the ALRS Volume 6. Part I covers NW Europe while Parts 2 and 3 cover the rest of the world. Obtainable from all good chart agents and marine bookshops, it is published at roughly 12-month intervals and updated every week in the Admiralty Weekly Notices to Mariners – which is free. Chart agents will happily mail the Notices if desired on a weekly monthly or quarterly basis but, although the document itself is free, packing and postage isn't so a charge will be made for the service. In general, ports and harbours operate on VHF only; very few have an MF facility

Coast Radio Stations

These act as shore-side telephone exchanges to link or 'patch' ships into the world-wide public telephone network – for a fee. Although there is no charge for talking *to* a Coast Radio Station, there is a charge for talking *through* one to the shore or another ship if it is beyond the range of the caller. For payment, an account must first be opened with the administration which operates the station(s) or an international radio accounting authority who will advise their AAIC (Accounting Authority Identification Code), Details are available from your national Radio Licensing Administration.

Most Coast Radio Stations use VHF; some use VHF and MF. The few on HF usually have MF and VHF too. Nearly all operate 24/7 and all speak English, the international language of travel. Full details in ALRS, Volume 1. Part 1 covers Europe, Africa and most of Asia; Part 2 covers the rest of the World.

NOTE All UK and most NW European Coast Radio Stations have closed but all Danish Coast Radio Stations and those in the Republic of Ireland remain operational as well as Ostend Radio (MF, HF, VHF) and Jersey Radio (VHF).

VHF Coast Radio Stations must be called directly on one of their working channels and addressed by their place-name plus the word 'Radio' as above. The exception is American MF and VHF stations where the words 'marine operator' are used instead of 'radio' e.g. 'Miami Marine Operator' (ALRS, Volume 1, Part 2).

Internet, e-mail and weather data can be obtained via a new HF station in USA. Details from SeaWave, Middletown, Rhode Island [www.seawave.com].

Although there are DSC frequencies for HF shore stations, they are usually called by voice directly on their main working channel in an appropriate band. In ALRS, this is indicated by their transmitting frequency in heavy type. In the '**RT (MF)**' and '**RT (HF)**' sections of the station entry, *their* transmit and *their* receive frequencies are tabulated under 'TRANSMITS' and 'RECEIVES'. *It is vital that these frequencies are reversed at the vessel. You receive on their transmit frequency and you transmit on their receiving frequency!* Under 'RT (HF)',the bracketed figures in italics are the ITU Channel Numbers for each pair of Duplex frequencies. Like VHF, these can be 'dialled-up' on modern SSB sets without being too concerned about the individual transmit and receive frequencies. Further columns give *their* transmit mode, transmitted power in kilowatts and watchkeeping hours *in GMT/UTC.* The full table of ITU channels is in Section A of Appendix 16 at the back of ALRS, Volume 1. The first figure or two gives the Band in MHz; the last two figures give the sequence. For example, Channel 410 is the tenth channel in the 4MHz Band and Channel 1205 is the fifth channel in the 12MHz Band (even though Coast Radio Stations transmit on 13MHz!). Delete the columns headed 'Assigned frequency' which are included just to confuse the uninitiated! For operators, the important column is headed 'Carrier frequency'.

Intership and MF working frequencies are not programmed into SSB sets as there are far too many. Instead, SSB sets include a number of blank channels which are easily programmed with a selection of intership Simplex frequencies (see Table 1) and MF pairs. Some anticipated ship-to-shore pairs could be entered before the trip starts then re-programmed as the journey progresses.

NOTE Vessels working *foreign* Coast Radio Stations transmit on 2045, 2048, 2051, 2054 or

Table 9.1 HF Intership (Simplex) Frequencies

4MHz Band	6MHz Band	8MHz Band	12MHz Band	16MHz Band	18/19MHz Band	22MHz Band	25/26MHz Band
4 146	6 224	8 294	12 353	16 528	18 825	22 159	25 100
4 149	6 227	8 297	12 356	16 531	18 828	22 162	25 103
	6 230		12 359	16 534	18 831	22 165	25 106
			12 362	16 537	18 834	22 168	25 109
			12 365	16 540	18 837	22 171	25 112
				16 543	18 840	22 174	25 115
				16 546	18 843	22 177	25 118

2057kHz so these can be programmed into the transmitter for starters. The receiving frequency can be entered when advised on 2182kHz.

Marinas, Yacht Harbours and Clubs

These must be called directly on a VHF working channel. British marinas use Ch.80. British yacht clubs use Ch.M for general use and Ch.M2 for race/regatta control. Only British yachts are licensed for these private channels. Full details of Marinas are in Admiralty Maritime Communications; NP289 for the UK and Med./Azores/Canaries, NP290 for the Caribbean and NP291 for UK and Baltic.

TECHNIQUE

On VHF, the initial Alert for all types of message and station should be by DSC on Channel 70. On MF, DSCindividual Alerts to Coast Radio Stations should be on 2189.5kHz in the absence of a national frequency. Otherwise by voice on a working channel VHF or 2182kHz, MF. On HF, the initial call is by voice on an appropriate working channel or Individual DSC Alert. See Appendix and ALRS, Vol. 1, Parts 1 or 2.

1. If a 'fist' microphone is being used, it should be held close to the mouth *but to one side*. If held directly in front, breath from the mouth causes rasping noises which blurs reproduction. If the user is right-handed, the microphone or telephone handset should be held in the left hand leaving the right hand free to operate the controls or make notes. (Most equipment is made for right-handed people.) The PTT switch may then be pressed.

2. Next, the attention of the other station must be attracted so it is addressed by name up to three times initially, e.g. "Ostend Radio, Ostend Radio". On VHF, it is usual to address shore stations once only, e.g. "Dover Coastguard". VHF signals tend to be 'loud and clear' or nothing. On HF, the maximum of 3 times may be necessary. If no reply, wait 3 minutes then try again or change bands.

3. The other station now needs to know who is calling so the calling station identifies itself (two or three times) by saying 'This is…'. Either the ship's name or callsign, spoken phonetically, may be used so a decision must be made before the PTT switch is pressed. It is usual to use the boat's name when calling other vessels which are known to the calling vessel. When calling strangers (most stations ashore), however, the callsign is by far the best method. It is extremely difficult to hear strange words (e.g. names) correctly at first, especially over a telephone or radio which introduces distortion. For example, the author once heard a yacht which sounded like 'Mary

Taylor' which was later spelled out as 'Merry Tiller'. Had the callsign been used, there would have been no confusion. *Marine callsigns are always spoken phonetically, in full.* Thus, it can be written down instantly by anyone of any nationality who may not even be able to pronounce the name. A secondary benefit is that the station's nationality is indicated by the first digit or two (details in ALRS Volume 1).

4. If a calling channel/frequency is being used, a suitable working channel or frequency should now be offered. (Although the station called dictates the working channel/frequency, time and confusion is saved if it is suggested by the caller).

5. Then the word 'over' to invite a reply. Then release the PTT switch.

6. If all is well, the station called will reply and indicate the working channel or frequency.

7. This must be acknowledged before the channel/frequency is changed, otherwise the called station will not know whether or not their transmission was heard.

8. The channel/frequency is now changed and the calling station waits for a call from the other station.

9. When communication has been re-established on the working channel/frequency, messages may now be passed.
    Note: Every time the PTT switch is pressed, the other station must be addressed (once) and the calling station identified (once) before the message is passed. If the callsign was used initially, time can be saved by giving the boat's name then spelling it out at this stage. (Thus, it pays to choose a short ship's name if possible.)

10. When business is finished, the calling station ends the conversation by identifying itself for the last time and concludes with the word 'out'. (Not, please 'over and out'; the phrase is contradictory and quite incorrect.)

11. Finally, both stations now re-tune to the calling channel/frequency.

When written out like this, R/T procedure looks very complex and rather daunting but in fact it is very simple and with a little practice becomes routine.

Having taught several thousand Marine R/T students over 30 years, the author found that the most common problem for many students was forgetting to address the other station and identify themselves *every time the button was pressed*.

For example, take a call from the author's ketch SILVINA, call sign 2JPG, to Portland Coastguard for weather and sea-state information:

On Channel 70:
Ideally, a DSC 'Routine' Alert to MMSI 002320012; otherwise…

On Channel 16:
Portland Coastguard;
This is Two, Juliet, Papa, Golf;
Two, Juliet, Papa, Golf;
Safety message, please;
Channel six-seven;
Over

Portland Coastguard replies, saying:

Two Juliet Papa Golf;
This is Portland Coastguard;
Channel six-seven and stand-by;
Over

Silvina then acknowledges, saying:

Portland Coastguard;
This is Two Juliet Papa Golf;
Channel six-seven and standing-by;
Over

The channel selector switch is then set to Channel 67.

On Channel 67, Portland Coastguard calls, saying:

Two Juliet Papa Golf;
This is Portland Coastguard;
Pass your message (or words to that effect);
Over

Silvina then replies, saying:

Portland Coastguard;
This is Two Juliet Papa Golf;
My ship's name is Silvina;
I spell: Sierra, India, Lima, Victor, India,
November, Alpha.
Please advise present conditions off Portland
Bill;
Over

Portland Coastguard answers, saying:

Silvina, this is Portland Coastguard;
Conditions off Portland Bill now are wind
South-Westerly six, sea very rough, visibility
ten miles;
Over

Silvina finally concludes the conversation by
saying:

Portland Coastguard; this is Silvina;
All copied; many thanks.
This is Silvina out

**The channel selector switch is then returned
to Channel 16.** A call to another yacht or
harbourmaster would be conducted in a very
similar manner.

On MF, a telephone call via a CRS
(e.g., Ostend Radio) is very similar…

On 2189.5kHz:
Ideally, a DSC 'Routine' call to MMSI
002050480; otherwise:

On 2182kHz:
Ostend Radio, Ostend Radio;
This is Two, Juliet, Papa, Golf;
Two, Juliet, Papa, Golf;
One telephone call; I have Two, Zero, Four,
Fife; Over

Ostend Radio replies, saying:

Two Juliet Papa Golf;
This is Ostend Radio;
Two Zero Four Fife for you;
Listen for me Two, Ait, Wun, Seven;
Turn number Wun;
Over

Silvina then acknowledges, saying:

Ostend Radio;
This is Two Juliet Papa Golf;
Listening Two Ait Wun Severn;
Turn number Wun;
Over

Silvina now tunes the *receiver (first)* to
2817kHz then the *transmitter* to 2045kHz **and
awaits a call from Ostend**. (New sets can
enter both frequencies into a Private Memory
channel) If capable, the set could now be
switched to DUPLEX operation.

On 2817kHz, Ostend Radio calls, saying:

Two Juliet Papa Golf;
This is Ostend Radio.
What have you for me?
(Or words to that effect!)
Over

On 2045kHz, Silvina replies giving all the
details for the telephone call:

Ostend Radio;
This is Two Juliet Papa Golf;
My ship's name is Silvina;
I spell: Sierra, India, Lima, Victor, India,
November, Alpha;
I have a call for:
Four, Four;
Wun, Niner, Zero, Tree;
Ait, Ait; Two, Two; Seven, Seven.My
Accounting Code is Golf Bravo Wun Four;
Over

Silvina would then be asked to 'Stand By'. The
ringing tone would soon be answered by the
correspondent who should be aware of the
Simplex system. The PTT button is then

pressed and conversation started. When the shore 'hangs-up', the charge stops and the ship is advised. Manual telephone calls are charged by the minute with a minimum charge of three minutes (but please also see the Section in Chapter 11 on Autolink).

NOTE: The 'Golf Bravo Wun Four' (GB14) quoted above indicates to any CRS that Silvina has an account with British Telecom through which payment is made. BT is one of 20 International Radio Accounting Authorities with whom British vessels may register. Details are enclosed with UK Ship's Licence Application Forms. All maritime countries have similar Radio Accounting Authorities.

SHORE TO SHIP CALLS

Full details will be found in the Telephone Directory. But, usually, it entails calling the exchange or a central booking clerrk on a freephone number and giving the boat's name, call sign, approximate position, name of person required and type of equipment (MF, HF or VHF). This information is then passed to the nearest Coast Radio Station who calls the ship immediately on HF, 2182kHz or Channel 16, VHF. If the call is not answered immediately or the vessel can only be reached on HF, the call is added onto a 'traffic list' which is broadcast every hour or two for the next 24 hours, after which it is dropped. If a reply is made immediately or to a traffic list, the shore number pays for the call. See ALRS Volume 1.

10

Satellites

The European CEPT Long Range Certificate (LRC) can include INMARSAT satellite use *provided* that a separate exam module is taken in addition to the basic LRC exam. If this is taken at the same time in the UK, there is no extra exam fee.

Short-wave SSB radiotelephones are relatively inexpensive and the Ionosphere is free but, being a natural phenomenon, can be erratic and unreliable. Skill and patience is needed and, even then, communication can be cut or severely disrupted for several hours. For difficulties or distress, this could be disastrous.

A more reliable alternative to the ionosphere for long-range **ship-to-shore communication** is to use four man-made 'mirrors in the sky'. Over 80 countries have formed a consortium called Inmarsat, Ltd. with headquarters in London to launch, maintain and control four communication satellites in geostationary orbit over the Equator. However, it is important to appreciate that satellites allow only one-to-one communication with the shore; in the

case of difficulty or distress, a general *broadcast* to nearby vessels cannot be made. So, satcom equipment *supplements* essential VHF and SSB radios.

Satellites remain in orbit because the centrifugal force of the orbit just balances the gravitational pull of the Earth. At low altitudes, the speed of orbit must be fast to counteract a fairly high gravitational force. For example, the Polar COPAS-SARSAT satellites complete an orbit in 1.5 hours. At higher altitudes, the speed of orbit is less. At a height of 22,300 miles (36,000km), the speed is such that an orbit takes 24 hours. If a satellite is put into orbit 22,300 miles above the Equator and in the same direction as the Earth's rotation, it appears to be stationary above a fixed point on Earth. Hence the term 'geo-stationary'.

One satellite serves the Pacific Ocean Region (POR), one serves the Indian Ocean Region (IOR), one is over a position just off the Ivory Coast of Africa (Atlantic Ocean Region East: AOR-E) and one is over Northern Brazil (Atlantic Ocean Region West: AOR-W). Between them and 37 Land Earth

Inmarsat's Mobile Satellite Communication Worldwide Coverage Map (© Inmarsat Ltd., 2001, Issue 5)

Key to the map:

Global beam coverage
- ········ Pacific Ocean Region
- ──── Atlantic Ocean Region-West
- ──── Atlantic Ocean Region-East
- ──── Indian Ocean Region
- ⬤ Land earth stations

Global Area Network and Inmarsat mini-M phone coverage
(for individual coverage areas of each ocean region please see reverse)

Extended Coverage Zones
for Inmarsat mini-M phone and Global Area Network low rate voice and data services

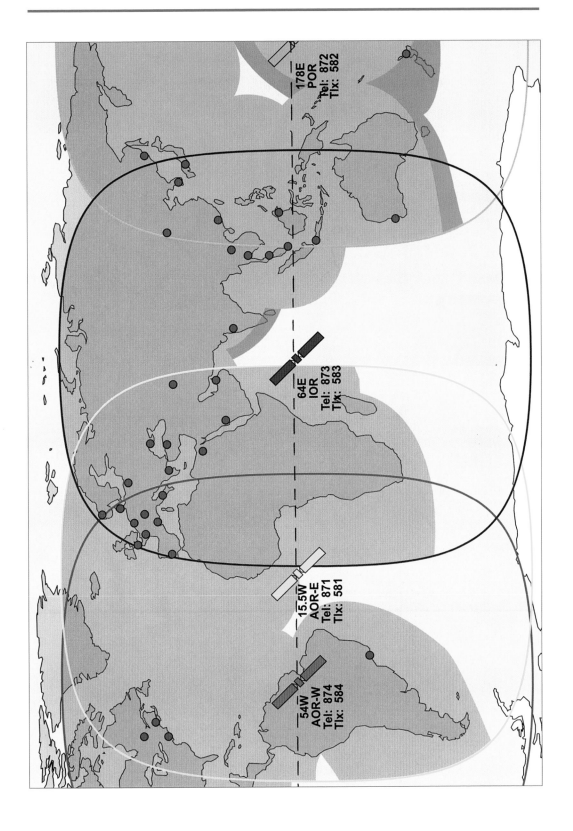

178E
POR
Tel: 872
Tlx: 582

64E
IOR
Tel: 873
Tlx: 583

15.5W
AOR-E
Tel: 871
Tlx: 581

54W
AOR-W
Tel: 874
Tlx: 584

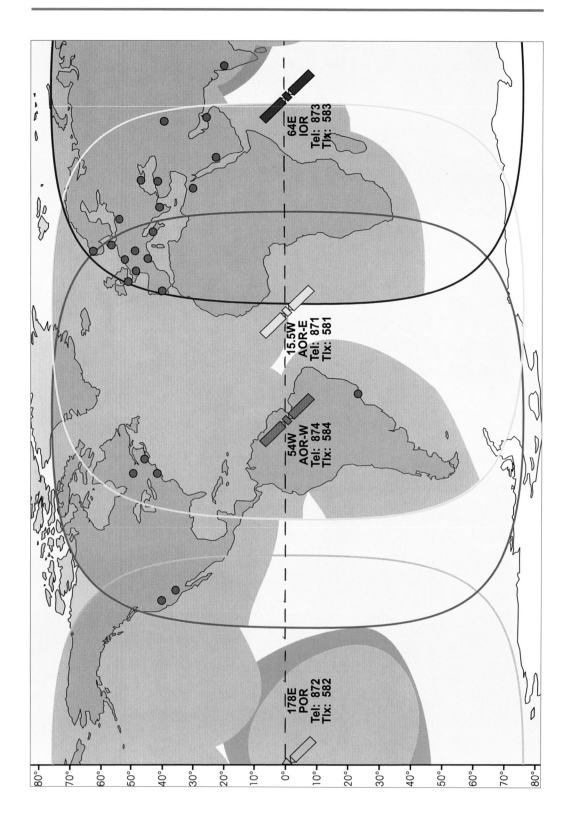

Stations (LES), they cover the whole World with large areas of overlap between 70°N and 70°S. At present INMARSAT offers six different systems:

INMARSAT-A
This 1982 analogue system is now superseded by INMARSAT-B.

INMARSAT-B
Digital technology gives higher quality speech, faster data rates, compressed video, a smaller (0.8m) dish and lower cost but still 'big ship' stuff.

INMARSAT-C
This is a text-only service for Telex, Fax and E-mail with superb reliability at any time and a price comparable with SSB. It works on a time-share basis with messages automatically sent in a succession of 32-character blocks (packets) interspersed with those of up to 21 other ships. At the end, the message is reassembled by a controlling station, then sent down the line. Thus, a two-way 'conversation' or Internet access is impossible. The charge is based on the number of blocks. Messages are passed directly to Telex or fax machines and computers ashore. From the shore, Telexes and e-mails can be sent directly to ships but text-only fax messages (hand-written or typed) must be sent via a Fax Bureau for an extra charge. The 30W transceiver is slightly larger than a VHF set; power requirements are low and no dish is required. The omnidirectional aerial/antenna is about the size of a 500g coffee can. A GPS can be combined or connected to the unit to provide an automatic position for Distress. Navtex-type information called SafetyNET is regularly broadcast and a vast database of information such as World news, sports results, exchange rates, share prices, etc. can be accessed. Approved for GMDSS, INMARSAT-C is well worthy of serious consideration for any ocean-going yacht *in addition* to essential VHF and SSB radios for free communication with other vessels, coastguards, harbours and general reception. www.inmarsat.com or Tel: +44 (0)20 7728 1777; Fax: +44 (0)20 7728 1142.

MINI-C
MINI–C is a new 2002 miniature version with the coverage and facilities of INMARSAT-C at lower cost **but not approved for GMDSS**.

INMARSAT-M
INMARSAT-M is a small version of INMARSAT-B giving low-cost speech, low-speed data, Internet, e-mail and fax facilities **but not approved for GMDSS**. With a 0.5m dish, it is suitable for small commercial vessels and large yachts.

MINI-M
MINI-M is a miniature version of INMARSAT-M using an A5-sized 'flat plate' aerial/antenna in a tiny dome. Most of the Northern Hemisphere is covered *but vast areas of Southern Hemisphere oceans are not.* **Not GMDSS approved**.

Iridium and Thuraya
Iridium and Thuraya are world-wide mobile 'phones using land-based cells where possible and Low Earth Orbit (LEO) satellites otherwise. Low-speed data, e-mail and Internet connections are also available. **Not GMDSS approved**.

Inmarsat's Mobile Satellite Communication Worldwide Coverage Map (© Inmarsat Ltd., 2001, Issue 5)

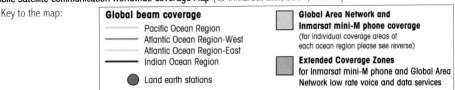

Key to the map:

Global beam coverage	Global Area Network and Inmarsat mini-M phone coverage
----------- Pacific Ocean Region	(for individual coverage areas of each ocean region please see reverse)
----------- Atlantic Ocean Region-West	
----------- Atlantic Ocean Region-East	Extended Coverage Zones
———— Indian Ocean Region	for Inmarsat mini-M phone and Global Area Network low rate voice and data services
● Land earth stations	

11

OTHER SERVICES

Although the main purpose of this book is to prepare students for the 'Long Range Certificate' exam, this chapter is included to introduce the small-boat sailor to the many other important services which are available in the world of Marine Radio but which do not form part of the exam syllabus. In addition to acting as communications stations for connecting ships into the public telephone system, the world's Coast Radio Stations also broadcast a vast amount of navigational and meteorological information. The possession of an SSB radiotelephone or even a good SSB receiver opens up a wide range of other services and facilities. Obviously, speech signals do not require any further equipment. Most meteorological and navigational information, though, is now broadcast in text or graphical form which requires additional equipment. Many long-distance sailors already possess a personal computer (PC) and this, with suitable software, can be plugged into the external loudspeaker socket of the SSB receiver or transceiver via a data-decode unit. This enables the information to be displayed on the screen, recorded on disk or printed.

All this broadcast information is freely available to anyone with suitable equipment but it is important that the yachting fraternity appreciate that *somebody* has to pay for it! Most of the information is intended for merchant ships who (eventually) pay for it by using the communication services to the shore or, in a roundabout way, through light dues. A few services are, strictly, military in which case we all contribute in taxes!

Weather Services

These are probably the most common and useful services used by both professional and leisure sailors. Weather information, which includes Gale Warnings and Storm Warnings, is disseminated in the forms of speech, printed text and graphically (maps/diagrams) over the three marine bands of MF, HF and VHF. Full details of all weather services for the whole World are contained in the *Admiralty List of Radio Signals* (ALRS), Vol. 3 which should be read in conjunction with the included diagrams. Published annually, ALRS is up-dated every week in Section VI of the Weekly Edition of the *Admiralty Notices to Mariners*, collected free from all Admiralty Chart Agents or by post for a small fee – see www.ukho.gov.uk.

Spoken Word

In addition to the regular weather forecasts given by domestic broadcasting stations, Coast Radio Stations and coastguard stations also broadcast regular weather forecasts specifically for mariners. Around the coasts of the UK, NW Europe and Mediterranean Sea, broadcasts by Coast Radio Stations are mostly on MF and/or VHF. Exceptions are Monaco Radio which broadcasts (in French and English) on HF and VHF, Hanko Radio (Finland) in English only on MF, HF & VHF and Rogaland Radio (Norway) in Norwegian and English on MF, HF & VHF Many other broadcasts are in English as well as their native language. British Coastguards broadcast a report every four hours (two hours above Force 6) on MF and VHF following an announcement on 2182kHz and Channel 16.

Around the coasts of North and South America, South Africa, India, Australasia, etc., broadcasts on HF are much more common. All US Coastguards broadcast on Channel 22CG; many on 2670kHz, MF and a few on HF. Around the USA coast, taped weather information is also continuously broadcast on special (private) 'Wx' Channels on VHF. See Chapter 6.

Printed Text (F1B)

A great deal of weather information is broadcast in text form on HF by using either the older RTTY (Radio Teletype) mode or the modern FEC (Forward Error Correction) mode. All text transmissions are termed Narrow Band Direct Printing (NBDP) and internationally classed as F1B. Two kinds of equipment can be plugged into the extension loudspeaker socket of an HF receiver or transceiver:

1. A laptop Personal Computer (PC) using a low-cost interface with suitable software, or
2. A dedicated self-contained printing terminal.
   Note: Any vessel with Radiotelex facilities already has the ability to decode FEC transmissions.

Facsimile (Weatherfax)

With a PC plugged into the extension loudspeaker socket of an SSB receiver or transceiver via a suitable decoder unit,

weather maps can be received just about anywhere in the World. Every day, a vast amount of weather information is broadcast in graphical form by about 90 stations around the globe. There are few areas of the globe not covered by these transmissions and this easy-to-interpret information is free to anyone with an HF SSB receiver or transceiver. Pictures transcend all language barriers so, wherever you are, current weather maps, forecast maps and sea-state charts are always available in a form that is easily understood. As the maps are transmitted simultaneously on several frequencies, some experiment is necessary for best results. Dedicated printing decoders may also be plugged into the receiver's extension loudspeaker socket. Once the equipment is set up, a built-in timer permits automatic reception at specific times. Then it is only necessary to tear off the printed information as required! Small, lightweight, dedicated weatherfax machines are also available.

STORM WARNINGS AND TIME SIGNALS

Information about Tropical Revolving Storms is broadcast by Navtex, SafetyNet (INMARSAT-C) and by voice from the two US National Bureau of Standards stations, WWV at Fort Collins, Colorado and WWVH at Kekaha in the Hawaiian Islands. These are Standard Frequency transmissions which also broadcast time signals every hour, on the hour; a male voice from WWV and a female voice from WWVH. Fort Collins transmits on 2500, 5000, 10000, 15000 & 20000kHz and broadcasts Storm Warnings for the NW Atlantic, Caribbean Sea, Gulf of Mexico and the North Pacific, east of 140°W. Kekaha duplicates the information for the North Pacific, east of 140°W but also covers the rest of the North Pacific and the South Pacific down to 25°S on the same frequencies as WWV except 20000kHz. Modulation is AMDSB (A3E). Full details are in ALRS Vol. 2 for time signals and Vol. 3 for weather services & navigational warnings.

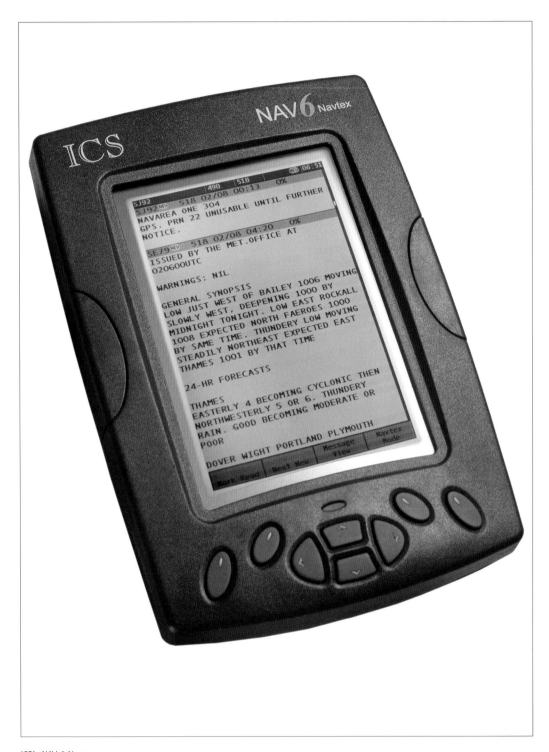

ICS's NAV 6 Navtex

NAVIGATIONAL WARNINGS

These are warnings of navigational hazards of a temporary or immediate nature, such as buoys off-station, lights unlit, radio beacons off-air, oil rigs under tow, seismic surveys, etc. Also included are warnings about irregular operation of electronic navaids. Like weather information, navigational warnings are also broadcast by voice on MF and VHF, by Telex on MF and HF and by NAVTEX on 518kHz and 490kHz at scheduled times. Obviously, it would take all day to broadcast details of every navigational hazard worldwide so the world is divided into sixteen NAVAREAS, each with its own transmitter(s). Time and frequency schedules are given under each station entry in ALRS Vol. 3.

Navtex

Forming an essential part of the GMDSS, this is an international system for broadcasting Maritime Safety Information (MSI) such as gale warnings, navigation warnings (including irregular operation of electronic and satellite navigation systems) weather forecasts, ice reports and SAR messages as printed text using NBDP/F1B. Transmitters are located at the sites of some (but not all) of the traditional MF Coast Radio Stations. Most popular coastal areas are covered except those of Australia and New Zealand due to the scarcity of MF Coast Radio Stations there. Non-Navtex coasts are covered by the equivalent INMARSAT-C SafetyNET service. For the English language, the primary international *assigned* frequency is 518kHz which gives a range of 100–500 miles from the transmitter. Additionally, there may also be local area or local language transmissions on 490kHz. (In the UK, the 490kHz broadcasts give the Inshore Waters forecast) In the Tropics, due to the much higher levels of 'static' interference on MF, the HF frequency of 4209.5kHz is also used. Although all stations use the same frequencies, mutual interference is avoided by operating the stations on a time-share basis. Within each

NAVAREA, each station is allocated a 10-minute slot every four hours. The transmission mode is Forward Error Correction (FEC) in which each character is transmitted twice to ensure a high level of reliability.

Ideally, the transmissions should be monitored continuously so a dedicated display or printing terminal is preferred. These take the form of a small box which contains the receiver, fixed-tuned to 518kHz, and an integral printing unit which disgorges roll paper through a slot in the front. They can be left switched-on permanently, taking little power in the stand-by mode. New sets will receive all messages from all stations but are easily programmed to reject all unwanted stations and some message types. Message types A, B, D and L (additional to A) cannot be rejected. The latest receivers are dual frequency.

For merchant ships, the Navtex receiver must be GMDSS-approved but non-approved (cheaper) Navtex receivers are available for non-SOLAS vessels.

Although a laptop PC with suitable software can be plugged into the extension loudspeaker socket of an SSB receiver or transceiver to receive Navtex, vital messages could be missed while the PC or radio are being used for other purposes. If using a standard SSB set on USB, tune it to 516.3kHz or 488.3kHz.

Each message carries a four-digit code: two letters and two figures. The first letter is the station identification, e.g. Niton (UK) is station 'S' but Niton also broadcasts navigational warnings at different times for adjacent area 'K' so, in the English Channel, both 'S' and 'K' should be selected. As there are more stations worldwide than alphabetical letters, each letter is used several times. Stations using the same ID letter are spaced sufficiently to avoid mutual interference.

The second letter indicates the type of

```
NAVTEX MESSAGE  ==================== SA71
WZ 320
ENGLAND. SOUTH COAST. APPROACHES TO
FALMOUTH. HELSTON LIGHTBUOY
50-05N 05-01W. MISSING. CANCEL WZ 041/98
(SA65)


NAVTEX MESSAGE  ==================== SA89
NAVAREA ONE 065.
BRISTOL CHANNEL, CELTIC SEA AND NORTH
EAST ATLANTIC OCEAN.
CABLE ROUTE CLEARANCE AND CABLE LAY IN
PROGRESS BY M/V EAS AND M/V
MAERSK DEFENDER ALONG ROUTE JOINING
OXWICH BAY 51-33N 04-07W, 51-24N
04-15W, 51-14N 07-26W, 50-20N 09-08W,
49-50N 18-45W, 50-00N 22-35W
AND 48-43N 29-41W.
WIDE BERTH REQUESTED.


NAVTEX MESSAGE  ==================== SA02
NAVAREA ONE 072
BRITISH ISLES, DIFFERENTIAL GPS.
TRANSMISSION OF CODED FORMAT DGPS
SIGNALS FROM UNITED KINGDOM AND
REPUBLIC OF IRELAND STATIONS WILL CEASE
ON 28 FEB 98. SIGNALS
RECEIVED AFTER THIS TIME WILL BE
UNRELIABLE AS TRANSMISSIONS WILL BE
DISCONTINUED WITHOUT NOTICE.


NAVTEX MESSAGE  ==================== SA03
WZ 396
DOVER STRAIT. VARNE LIGHTVESSEL 51-01N
01-24E, RACON UNRELIABLE.


NAVTEX MESSAGE  ==================== SA04
WZ 397
DOVER STRAIT. ZC1 LIGHTBUOY 50-45N
01-27E UNLIT.
```

Examples of Navtex messages

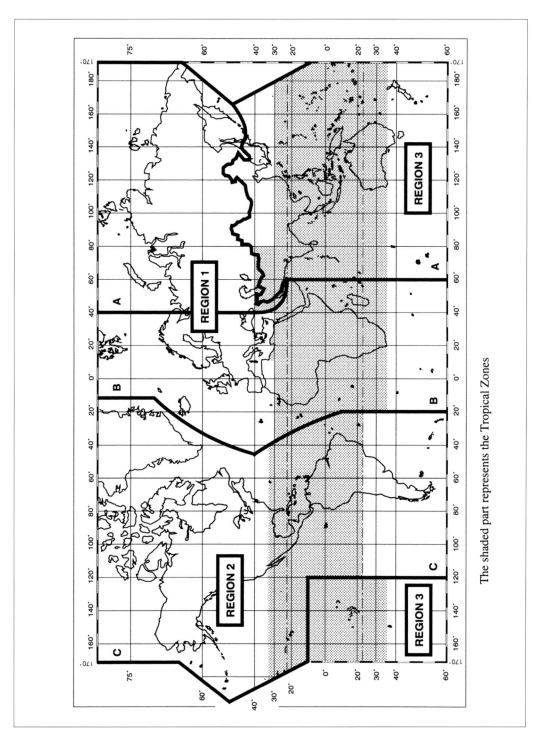

World Radio Regions for the allocation of frequencies. The shaded part represents the Tropical Zones. From *Maritime Mobile Manual* (1996 edition) page RR8–2.

message, e.g., A = Navigational Warnings, B = Meteorological Warnings, C = Ice Reports, D = SAR Information, etc.

The two figures are a nominal serial number from 01 to 99. After 99, the series re-starts at 01 but avoiding messages still in force. Over a 3-day period, messages already received on dedicated printing terminals will not be reprinted. Serial Number 00 is reserved for very urgent messages which are broadcast immediately on receipt, sounding an alarm in the receiver.

Full details are published in ALRS Vols. 3 and 5. Full instructions for using dedicated equipment are included with the set.

Time Signals

In addition to WWV and WWVH mentioned under Storm Warnings, many other stations broadcast time signals. Their methods of indicating time differ greatly; non of them as easy as the Greenwich 'pips'. Refer to ALRS Vol. 2.

Text Communication Services (Telex, Fax and E-mail)

The technology is called Narrow Band Direct Printing (NBDP) and classified internationally as F1B. The first marine radio text service was Radiotelex or Telex Over Radio (TOR) for communicating with teleprinter machines ashore but the term 'Telex' now includes the other text systems of fax and e-mail. At the vessel, the transmission system is common to all three, only the address is different. With the addition of a laptop PC, suitable software and a special modem (MOdulator/DEModulator) connected to a suitable (or suitably-modified) Marine SSB, printed text can be sent and received by Telex, Fax or E-mail via many automated MF and HF Coast Radio Stations worldwide. If the recipient ashore lacks the appropriate technology, the message can be delivered by post.

Telex and e-mail messages are automatically routed straight through enabling a 'conversation' to be held with an operator ashore if desired. If the message cannot be delivered for any reason, it is stored in an electronic 'mailbox' to await retrieval by the recipient at a convenient time. Messages to fax machines, however, are always routed through a 'store and forward' system. When the Telex is received by the CRS, it is automatically converted into fax form and sent to the number given. If the fax cannot be delivered for any reason, repeated attempts are made during the next 24 hours. If the message still cannot be delivered, the vessel is freely advised. The message and charge are then cancelled.

Using a PC, the whole message, complete with its numerous command codes, can be prepared well in advance of the actual transmission time so there is no need to hurry. As much time as necessary can be spent with preparation. When all is ready, the whole sequence of establishing contact with the Coast Radio Station and sending the message can be initiated with a few simple keystrokes.

Free Telex messages may also be exchanged directly with other suitably-equipped ships within range using dedicated single-frequency channels in the MF and HF bands. (As with R/T, Coast Radio Stations use two-frequency channels for Telex, too). If the other ship is out of range or, simply, not listening, Telex messages may be sent via a Coast Radio Station using the store-and-forward system for which there is a charge. **Note**: The two-frequency Coast Radio Station channels cannot be used for intership communication by Telex or R/T.

Text messages are much cheaper than radiotelephone calls via a CRS which charges by the minute with a minimum charge of three minutes. Text messages are charged in 6-second increments. Although slower and less convenient, the service is more reliable than R/T and the recipient receives printed text. To participate in the text service, an

This Barrett 923 HF set linked to a laptop PC can be used to send e-mails and access the internet

account must first be opened with the company operating the Coast Radio Station(s). They supply detailed instructions for using the system. Many major companies operating this service have reciprocal agreements with each other so it is not necessary to open multiple accounts! In case of difficulty with the text system, an operator can always be called upon for free assistance. Distress and Medico (medical advice/assistance) calls are freely connected to the appropriate service.

The NBDP system could be described as automated Morse whereby the character-code is formed automatically by simply pressing a button on a digital keyboard. Obviously, this requires much less skill than tapping a Morse key! However, the code is much more complex since it uses a combination of audible tones for each character. Only two tones are used: 1,615kHz and 1,785kHz (i.e. 1.7kHz ± 85Hz) which gives rise to the characteristic "chirp-chirp" sound when heard by loudspeaker. In English, the system is called Frequency Shift Keying (FSK) and internationally designated F1B.

Because only sine-wave tones are used, the transmitter is being used at maximum efficiency the whole time. With speech, the transmitter only gives its full output on occasional peaks; the average output is only about one quarter its maximum! Due to the much greater efficiency of digital technology, much less power is required; in many cases, the transmitter can be set to its lowest power level without degrading the reliability of communication; 30 watts of F1B has been found to be as effective as 120 watts of J3E. Full-power digital operation severely tests the power supply and, if continued for more than a few minutes, requires the help of the generator (see Chapter 5). Many traditional HF Telex stations are now closed but a new company has established a World-wide station on Rhode Island, USA. Details on www.seawave.com or tyoung@seawave. com.

Most HF SSB transceivers can be used for

text communication although older sets may require modification to reduce the transmit/receive switching times. This is because an error-correcting **A**utomatic **R**epetition **Q**uery (ARQ) system is used. The transmitting station sends the message in groups of three characters. A special character-code is used which enables the receiving station to check whether or not it has received all the characters correctly. If all is well, the receiving station sends an 'OK' signal ('handshake') then the transmitting station continues with the next three characters. If a group is received incorrectly, the receiving station requests a repetition until it receives the group correctly. The group of three characters can be repeated up to 32 times before the system gives up! The transmit/ receive change-over time required at each station is less than 50mS which is why some older transceivers need modification. The error-correcting ARQ system ensures that, even with poor signals, errors are rare. In fact, ARQ signals get through when speech signals will not. (Radio Amateurs use a very similar system called AMTOR.)

Most of the Telex channels, over 250, are in the HF Band but there are some in the MF Band. They are mostly two-frequency channels (like the ship-to-shore R/T channels) with the transmitter and receiver on different frequencies. There are also a few single-frequency channels designated for intership operation.

When not handling Telex traffic, most Coast Radio Stations broadcast a 'channel free' signal. This incorporates the station call-sign in Morse code with several characteristic bird-like 'chirp-chirps' repeated continously. The Morse speed is only about 5 words per minute (like RDF beacons) so recognition is easily learned. This makes it easy to choose the best channel in the prevailing conditions – simply check all channels and select the loudest! (ALRS. Vol. 1)

Note: When manually tuning all F1B signals such as Telex, Navtex, etc., with an ordinary SSB receiver, 1.7kHz must be subtracted from

the published transmit frequency. The reason is that, whereas R/T frequencies are designated by their suppressed carrier, F1B transmissions are designated by their 'assigned' frequency (centre of the transmitted bandwidth) which is 1.7kHz above the (also suppressed) carrier. This 'offset', as it is called, must be subtracted from the published transmit frequency, otherwise nothing will be heard. When transmitting with a dedicated modem and software, the offset is automatically subtracted. With a modern, computer-controlled transceiver, tuning is entirely automatic. **Note**: If tuning Telex transmissions just to assess propagation conditions, 1.5kHz is more easily subtracted mentally.

Most shore Telex stations are computerized so that messages from the shore can be retrieved from a 'mailbox' when the vessel next calls in. Traffic lists are often accompanied by weather forecasts and other general information. Broadcasts are in FEC mode so only the receiver is used. with no 'handshake'.

In addition to two-way messaging, shore stations permit vessels to converse directly with an operator or doctor in an emergency and some give access to a variety of databases such as weather forecasts, sports results, currency exchange rates, Optimum Traffic Frequency (OTF) guides, Navigational Warnings, etc.

Full instructions for using the system are provided by the CRS operating company but essential information such as Telex stations, frequencies, watch-keeping hours, command codes, etc. is published in ALRS Vol. 1 and the new *Admiralty Maritime Communications* directories. These three volumes are a compendium of all marine radio services for the popular sailing areas of the British Isles & Baltic, British Isles & Mediterranean and Azores/Canaries & Caribbean.

With the advent of the PC, text communication has become much cheaper and easier to use in recent years and is worthy of serious consideration by the long-distance sailor. Text communication by radio is far more reliable than speech although less convenient. Not only is more efficient use made of the transmitted power, the bandwidth is much less, allowing more channels to be accommodated in the radio spectrum. Also, since the amount of received background noise is proportional to receiver bandwidth, a narrower signal means that a greater proportion of signal to noise is possible.

Thus, text communication produces louder, clearer signals. As we saw in Chapter 2, SSB speech occupies a bandwidth of 3kHz and this cannot be reduced without seriously degrading intelligibility. Thus, R/T channels are spaced at 3kHz intervals. Telex channels, however, are spaced at 0.5kHz intervals; this means that 6 Telex channels can occupy the space of one R/T channel and the amount of received noise is 1/6th of R/T. Text messages cost much less than R/T and the recipient gets a clear, hard copy without the sender having to spell the whole message through bad interference. For serious, reliable, cheap long-distance marine radio, Telex/Fax/E-mail is a 'must'.

Morse code occupies even less space in the radio spectrum. A hand-sent Morse signal is barely 30Hz wide so 100 Morse signals can be sent for every speech signal and the amount of noise received is 100 times less! Marine Radio was founded on sending on/off digits by a skilled operator with a Morse key but in 1999, after 100 years, it was the last professional service to use it. American Samuel Morse's wonderful invention of 1837 now relies solely on Radio Amateurs to keep those skills alive although even this is now in doubt. Marine Radio now uses less-skilled, but faster, electronically-generated digits for text messages.

Shore-To-Ship

The system works almost as well in reverse. Text mesages can be sent to suitably-

equipped ships from the shore. E-mail and Telex messages are routed straight through to the ship in ARQ (conversation) mode provided the vessel has lodged watchkeeping details with the company operating the Coast Radio Station. Otherwise, the message goes into an electronic 'mailbox' for storage to await collection by the vessel at a convenient time. Text messages may also be dictated by telephone to a Coast Radio Station.

Faxes can also be sent to ships but only as text although they may be typed or hand written. Graphics cannot be sent. Upon receipt by the Coast Radio Station, the message is manually transcribed onto a PC in a form acceptable for digital transmission. Because an operator is involved, an extra service charge is added to the transmission charge. Full details from your telephone company.

Autolink and Mobile Phones

In the early 90s, an Italian company, CIMAT (pronounced 'chee-mat'), invented the Autolink system of direct dialling into the Public Switched Telephone Network (PSTN) via participating Coast Radio Stations in the MF, HF and VHF Bands. Many countries are now equipped. A special modem or handset is plugged into the microphone socket of a standard *Duplex* set. There is even a model allowing 'scrambled' (secret) transmissions. The equipment is fairly expensive but, because the system is fully automatic, the call rate is slightly cheaper and the minimum period is only one minute. Coast Radio Station operating companies can advise. It is the Maritime radio answer to cellphones but with much greater range when using MF and HF and without the monthly charge.

Cellular telephones, operating around 900MHz, can be used in many inshore waters but, even with high-mounted external aerials, their range is the same 'line of sight' range as marine VHF; much less than MF or HF. However, they are more convenient, give a fair degree of security and much cheaper calls than VHF.

CAUTION
In emergencies, cellphones are no substitute for marine VHF although they are better than nothing. Direct contact with coastguards may be possible through the UK 999, Continental 112 or USA 911 service but other vessels nearby who may be able to help, will not be aware of the situation. You cannot communicate with SAR aircraft or lifeboat by cellphone and they cannot take direction-finding bearings on cellphones as they can with VHF.

Recently, several World-wide mobile 'phone systems using dozens of cross-connected Low Earth Orbit (LEO) satellites have appeared on the market. Most notable are Iridium and Thuraya. See also Chapter 10.

12

CB and

AMATEUR RADIO

Firstly, it must be emphasised that although Amateur Radio and CB are most useful adjuncts to professional Marine Radio, they are not alternative systems. Amateur Radio is a technical hobby; a person-to-person fun activity. Licensed Amateurs may only communicate with other licensed Amateurs (who may be ahore or afloat) 'on matters relating to technical investigations or remarks of a personal nature'. *Messages for third parties are strictly prohibited.* (Exceptionally, in Britain, Radio Amateurs are allowed to pass third party messages for essential 'user services' such as Police, Ambulance, Red Cross, the Saint John Ambulance Brigade, etc., in case of emergency.) However, as *any* frequency including Amateur frequencies may be used for distress, these could be tried if all else failed.

In Britain, at least, the general public seem to be confused as to the difference (if any) between Radio Amateurs (as they are properly called) and CB operators, lumping them both together as radio 'hams'. Although both activities are concerned with radio communication as a personal convenience or hobby, they are quite different.

Citezens Band (CB)

This started in the USA soon after the Second World War as an unlicensed, unregulated short range radio communication system for non-technical, unqualified people on the move such as truckers, taxi drivers, farmers, etc., who were unable to use the public telephone system. A small band of frequencies around 27MHz, right at the top end of the HF band and using AM, was chosen by the Federal Communications Commission (FCC), the regulatory body in the USA. The equipment has to be professionally made to an approved standard and the usual ITU (International Telecommunications Union) prohibitions such as foul language apply but, these apart, it is a free-for-all service. Operators make up their own identifying 'handle' which is not registered and cannot, therefore, be traced.

Gradually, American CB sets were imported illegally into Britain and other European countries causing interference to established and essential services. The number involved and the fact that most operators were mobile made prosecution difficult so CB was legalized in Britain in 1981. Forty numbered channels between 27.6MHz and 27.99MHz are also used in Britain and Europe but frequency modulation (FM) is used and the Continental frequencies are slightly different so early British CB sets were incompatible with all other European countries. However, eighty-channel dual-frequency sets with both UK and Continental frequencies are now

An ICOM IC-756PROII Transceiver often used by Amateur Radio Specialists

available in the UK. Hand-held versions of these new sets can be taken on Continental holidays and those living in SE England may sometimes be able to talk to the French from home! CB is ideal for boat-to-boat chatting instead of using the VHF which has only four intership channels. Many clubs find CB ideal for controlling rescue boats – the equipment is cheap and simple to operate without exams. Currently in the UK, a licence must be bought but deregulation is planned for July, 2004, *using European frequencies only.*

AMATEUR RADIO

This is a different 'ball game' altogether. Unfortunately, the word 'amateur' is usually (but, in this case, wrongly) taken to mean unskilled, inept or incompetent. In this context, however, 'amateur' means the same as it does in sport, i.e., the activity is enjoyed purely as a pastime, not for financial gain but the person is no less an expert. Radio Amateurs are radio experts as those who sit the exams quickly discover! (Nevertheless, the possession of an Amateur Radio Licence does not qualify the holder to operate professional marine or aviation radios without first passing the appropriate exam!) Amateur Radio (with capital letters) is a highly technical international service recognized and regulated by the International Telecommunications Union (ITU) for the self-training of the licensee. Regulation, however, brings with it many rights and privileges – some unique.

The equipment may be home-designed and built whereas all professional equipment must be factory-built to an approved standard. But, because Amateur equipment must also be built to the same high standard to avoid causing interference to essential services (some of the Amateur Bands actually share parts of the Marine Band), holders of a Full Licence must be technically qualified to undertake this design and manufacture. Consequently, a high-standard technical exam in radio engineering principles and radio regulations must be passed.

In the UK, there are three grades of licence, Foundation, Intermediate and Full. The Foundation Licence is awarded after a 12-hour assessed course held over several weekends at local Amateur Radio clubs authorised by the Radio Society of Great Britain (RSGB), the national association. These clubs also offer 30-hour courses for the Intermediate licence for which (pro tem) the RSGB holds monthly exams at local radio clubs. Since 1946, the Radio Amateur's Exam (RAE) for the Full Licence, was held in May and December by the City and Guilds of London (CGLI) at the Institute, many local Technical Colleges and overseas but their last RAE will be/was held in December, 2003. From 2004, a new Examination Body will be appointed which could be the RSGB. (Please see their website at www.rsgb.org.) Candidates for the Intermediate exam must have passed the Foundation course and from 2004, candidates for the Full RAE will need to have passed the Intermediate exam. So, from 2004, the RAE may only be sat by having previously passed two stages of formal, *practical* instruction for a total of at least 42 hours.

In many cases, there are no nationality requirements for the technical exam. The several grades of American FCC exam and Morse test can be taken in the UK. (RSGB address in Appendix or see www. rsgb.org)

Once qualified, a unique, international, *personal* callsign is allocated. This contrasts with all professional radio stations where the callsign identifies the ship, aircraft or shore station. Traditionally, UK Amateur callsigns were not re-issued; they usually died with the owner. In future, however, a 'long-dead' callsign may be re-issued due to a foreseeable shortage. As the first digit (or two) indicates the nationality (and, ashore, the rough location) of the station, many countries have reciprocal arrangements with others to issue their own licence and callsign to ex-patriots on the strength of that of another participating country.

To indicate operation at sea (with the Master's permission), the spoken call-sign is modified by the addition of the words 'maritime mobile'. This makes the station very special and attractive to Radio Amateurs ashore.

Relatively high power (several hundred watts) is allowed which can give World-wide range compared with the few watts allowed for CB. Some countries such as the USA and Canada even allow 1kW.

No specific frequencies are allocated, merely limits to about 20 bands distributed throughout the entire radio spectrum – eight are within the long-range HF Band. Operation is permitted on any frequency within the specified limits.

This is why only Amateur transceivers have Variable Frequency Oscillators (VFO's) on both the transmit and receive side whereas CB and professional radio-telephones can only transmit on a range of specific, spot frequencies.

❏ A wide range of modes may be used such as speech (AM, FM, SSB), Morse code, TV (still and moving pictures), data, Telex, facsimile, etc.
❏ Many of the Amateur Bands are allocated by the ITU on a primary, exclusive basis and complaints can be made against unauthorized intruders.

EQUIPMENT

Like any other work, the correct tools should be used for the job in hand and this philosophy also applies to radio. Ideally, therefore, if both marine Radio and Amateur Radio operation is desired, dedicated equipment for each task should be obtained. As very similar frequencies are involved, the same aerial can be used and, if both sets are from the same stable, probably the same ATU to save a substantial sum.

In theory, Amateur Radio equipment also seems capable of being used on the Marine frequencies and, being cheaper, makes it very attractive. This is not so, however, for several reasons:

● On the transmitting side, Amateur equipment is inhibited so that it will only transmit on licensed Amateur bands.
● Although this inhibition can be removed on some Amateur equipment, few sets have the twin variable frequency oscillators (VFOs) necessary for two frequency operation on the Marine public correspondence channels.
● The frequency accuracy and stability of most Amateur SSB sets is well below the high standard required on Marine frequencies. The standard required of Marine sets is ±10Hz whereas the average Amateur set is within 100Hz which is the bare minimum for SSB operation.
● A proper Marine callsign will not be allocated for Amateur equipment and public telephone calls cannot be made with an Amateur callsign. (Exception: calls *within the USA* can be made via a local US Amateur).
● Unlike proper Marine Radio, Amateur

Radio equipment is not made to go to sea. Proper Marine Radio is also inhibited to prevent transmission on unauthorised frequencies but the inhibition can often be removed by the supplier provided that an Amateur Radio Licence can be shown. With the transmitter section 'broadbanded', marine transceivers will operate on the main long distance Amateur Bands although a little less conveniently than dedicated Amateur equipment, so this is the route to take. Choose a Marine transceiver in which the transmit frequency is user-programmable (some are not) and, for preference, the receiver section should have continuously-variable tuning (some have not).

The technique for using Marine SSB sets on the Amateur bands is to firstly tune in the station on the receiver, note the frequency, then programme the transmit and receive frequency into the memory channel on that same frequency (Amateurs normally operate in the simplex mode using one frequency). If the set has continuously variable tuning on the receive side, it may be possible for a specialist to modify the set to connect this control to the transmit side as well. The situation is eased if Amateur operation is confined to the Maritime Mobile nets which do operate on specific spot frequencies.

Note:
Although most Marine SSB sets will operate on the main long distance HF Amateur bands of 14MHz, 21MHz and 28MHz (after modification), they will not usually operate on *all* the HF Amateur bands. The reason for this is that the three lower frequency Amateur bands (1.8MHz, 3.5MHz and 7MHz) are used on the lower sideband whereas Marine R/T uses the upper sideband only and most Marine SSB sets will only transmit on the upper sideband.

For a free booklet entitled *'How To Become A Radio Amateur'*, write to the (UK) Radiocommunications Agency, Wyndham House, 189, Marsh Wall, London, E14 9SX Tel: 020 7211 0211, Fax: 020 7211 0507 (Website: www.radio.gov.uk). Or contact your own national society.

For a free Information Pack on UK Amateur Radio, write to: The Radio Society of Great Britain (RSGB), Lambda House, Cranborne Road, Potters Bar, Herts., EN6 3JE, Tel: 0870 904 7373 , Fax: 0870 904 7374 (Website: www.rsgb.org; e-mail: sales@rsgb.org.uk). Or your own national society.

Some Maritime Mobile Nets (Subject to change)

UK/MM NET: 14,303kHz at 08.00Z, G4FRN (Bill) and 18.00Z, G4YZH (Bruce).

TRANSATLANTIC; (crossing season) 21,400kHz at 13.00Z, 8P6QM, Trudi in Barbados.

INTERMAR; 14,300kHz at 06.00 to 11.00Z but **CYPRUS NET**; 09.00-10.00Z.

AUSTRALIA, N.Z. and AFRICA NET: (South Pacific & Indian Ocean), 21,200kHz at 05.00Z.

BAY OF ISLANDS NET; (S. Pacific, Australia and N.Z.), 3,820kHz at 07.15Z; 14,329kHz at 19.00Z.

WATERWAYS NET; (US East Coast Waterways & Caribbean), 7,628kHz at 11.45Z.

NB, 'Z' means GMT/UTC

13

The International

Phonetic Alphabet

For accuracy in communication, it is absolutely vital that every radio or telephone operator is fluent in the phonetic alphabet. When speaking over the radio or telephone, it can be almost impossible for the correspondent to distinguish between 'F' and 'S', 'N' and 'M' or 'B', 'D', 'P' and 'T'. For accuracy, names and uncommon words should be spelled-out

Letter	Word	Spoken as	Variations
A	ALPHA	AL-fah	
B	BRAVO	BRA-voh	
C	CHARLIE	CHAR-lee	French may say 'SHAR-lee'
D	DELTA	DELL-tah	
E	ECHO	ECK-oh	
F	FOXTROT	FOKS-trot	
G	GOLF	GOLF	
H	HOTEL	hoh-TELL	French may say 'oh-TELL'
I	INDIA	IN-dee-ah	
J	JULIET	JEW-lee-ETT	Germans may say 'YOU-lee-ett'
K	KILO	KEE-loh	
L	LIMA	LEE-mah	
M	MIKE	MIKE	
N	NOVEMBER	no-VEM-bah	
O	OSCAR	OSS-kar	
P	PAPA	pa-PAH	
Q	QUEBEC	key-BECK	
R	ROMEO	ROW-mee-oh	
S	SIERRA	see-AIR-rah	
T	TANGO	TANG-go	
U	UNIFORM	YOU-nee-form	
V	VICTOR	VIK-tah	
W	WHISKEY	WISS-key	Germans may say 'VISS-key'
X	X-RAY	ECKS-ray	
Y	YANKEE	YANG-key	
Z	ZULU	ZOO-loo	

using an easily-recognizable word for each letter.

This technique originated in the First World War with the 'Ack-Ack', 'Beer-Beer' system but has changed several times since then. The current alphabet was originally devised for use by NATO in the 1950's but is now used universally.

Note: When spelling out words phonetically, it is essential to say **'I spell'** before launching into phonetics; this is a signal for the recipient to put pencil to paper and take down the message.

Numeral	Spoken as:
32	TREE TOO
459	FOW-er, FIFE, NINE-er
200	TOO, ZERO, ZERO
8162	AIT, WUN, SIX, TOO
7000	SEV-en TOUSAND
2.5	TOO POINT FIFE

Phonetic Numerals

There is also a system of International phonetic numerals but it is rarely used as most communicators throughout the world say numerals in English. However, there is still some possibility of confusion, particularly with 'five' and 'nine', so it is usual to shorten 'five' to 'fife' and extend 'nine' to 'niner' to help distinguish between them.

Numeral	Spoken as:
1	WUN
2	TOO
3	TREE
4	FOW-er
5	FIFE
6	SIX
7	SEV-en
8	AIT
9	NIN-er
0	ZERO

Do not say 'oh' for '0' (nought or zero) as it can sound like 'two'. Numbers should be spoken figure by figure except for whole thousands and if a decimal point occurs in a number, it is given as 'point'.

IMPORTANT PROcedural Words [PRO Words]

MAYDAY   DISTRESS call for YOURSELF

MAYDAY RELAY Distress call on behalf of someone else

PAN–PAN   Indicates an URGENT call concerning the SAFETY of a SHIP or PERSON [e.g., man overboard]

PAN–PAN MEDICO or PAN–PAN RADDIO MAY-DEE-CAL
Precedes a call to a *Coast Radio Station* requesting urgent medical advice. You will then be given a free telephone call to a doctor in the Accident & Emergency Department [A&E] of a local hospital.
Note: French Doctors, in the main, only speak French; in otther countries, many have a command of English

SEELONCE MAYDAY
Radio Silence on Channel 16 or 2182kHz is imposed by the Station controlling DISTRESS COMMUNICATIONS using this phrase. Silence should be observed automatically during a DISTRESS Situation

SEELONCE DISTRESS
RADIO SILENCE ON CHANNEL 16 OR 2182KHZ imposed by ANY station OTHER than the one CONTROLLING Distress Communications

PRUDENCE   A concession, at the discretion of the CONTROLLING station, to allow essential signals on Channel 16 or 2182kHz – even though a DISTRESS situation may not be fully concluded

SEELONCE FEENEE
End of radio silence

SÉCURITÉ [SAY–CURE–EE–TAY]
Safety signal to indicate that a message of NAVIGATIONAL IMPORTANCE is about to start

SAY AGAIN   REPETITION required

ALL AFTER   Everything FOLLOWING the word or phrase indicated

ALL BEFORE Everything PRIOR to the word or phrase indicated

ALL BETWEEN
Everything BETWEEN the words or phrases indicated

WORD AFTER, WORD BEFORE, WORD BETWEEN
as above

STATION CALLING
[Your ship's name or call-sign] Form of address to station which has called you but whose identification is in doubt. If, on the other hand, you *think* someone is calling YOU, *do nothing*, but wait for the other station to repeat the call

OVER   Invitation to the other person to transmit

OUT   End of conversation.
Note: As the words 'OVER' & 'OUT' are contradictory; **it is NOT correct to end a transmission with 'OVER-AND-OUT'**

CORRECTION
The last word or phrase was wrong. This should be followed by 'I SAY AGAIN…'

READ BACK Repeat the message you have just received for confirmation tht it was received correctly

RADIO CHECK
Tell me the strength & quality of my signal

I SPELL   I am about to spell the word just said in the International Phonetic Alphabet

Glossary

AAIC – Accounting Authority Identification Code; payment for public telephone calls (see GB14)

AF – Audio Frequencies; 20Hz-20kHz

AFSK – Audio Frequency Shift Keying: the technique used for digital transmissions which is particularly of use for Telex messages. Internationally designated F1B

AIS/UAIS – (Universal) Automatic Identification System: Identification of ships by interrogating their VHF set

ALRS – The *Admiralty List of Radio Signals*, the primary source of all information regarding Marine radio stations, frequencies etc. Available from Admiralty Chart Agents

AM/AMDSB – Amplitude Modulated Double Sideband: full carrier. Used for domestic broadcasting

AMTOR – The Amateur Radio version of TOR (Telex Over Radio)

AMVER – Automated Mutual Assistance Vessel Rescue System: a 'reporting in' system for recording the positions of participating vessels, providing a last known position in case of an incident

ARQ – Automatic Error Request: an automated error checking and correction system between transmitter and receiver

asl – Above Sea Level: height of VHF aerials above sea level

ATU – Aerial Tuning Unit, without which the communicator's life would be very difficult – see Chapter 5

Authority to Operate – Normally granted when the radio operator passes the examination for the *Certificate of Competence in Radio-telephony*

Autolink – Allows automatic ship to shore telephone connection on MF, HF & VHF, with the option of scrambled traffic for privacy

A3E – International classification of AM/AMDSB

Callsign – Sequence of letters and/or figures allocated to a radio-equipped vessel, aircraft or shore station e.g., MGHV4. Always spelt out phonetically over the air, it is less prone to misinterpretation than the vessel's name

Capture Effect – On VHF, the radio locks onto the strongest signal and reproduces that to the exclusion of all others

CB – Citizen's Band radio: the unqualified 'free for all' band

CEPT – Conference of European Posts & Telegraph Administrations: the European Unions' communications regulatory authority

Certificate of Competence in Radiotelephony Granted to operators who have passed the appropriate examination. This is mandatory for ALL operators of marine radiotelephones

Channel 16 – The VHF calling and distress channel

Channel M – A private channel used by British yachts and yacht clubs and by those British marinas which have not yet converted to using Channel 80 (the British marina channel)

Clarifier – A very fine tuning control used to match the receiver's re-inserted carrier exactly to the other station's transmitter frequency

Coast Radio Station (CRS) – Shore-based 'telephone exchange' which links radio equipped vessels with the international telephone system

CROSSMA – The French Coastguard Service for the English Channel

D/F or RDF – Radio direction-finding

DSC – Digital Selective Calling. New system of Calling and Distress Alerting by digital signals - not voice

Dual Watch – Electronic device fitted to marine VHF sets allowing two channels (Channel 16 and another selected channel) to be monitored at once

Duplex – Dual frequency system allowing simultaneous two-way conversation by radio

EMC – Electromagnetic Compatibility: the technique for reducing electronic interference

EPIRB – Emergency Position-Indicating Radio Beacon. Automatic distress alerting and location device by satellite

FEC – Forward Error Correction: a transmission mode in which each character is transmitted twice to ensure a high level of reliability. Used for text broadcasts

FM – Frequency Modulation. The system by which signals are transmitted on the Marine VHF band

GB14 – The account code of British Telecom, one of many Accounting Authorities which must be used when making international telephone calls

GHz – Gigahertz: one thousand Megahertz. INMARSAT uses 1.6GHz

GMDSS – The Global Maritime Distress and Safety System: the GMDSS gives world-wide safety coverage using MF, HF, VHF and satellites

gt – Gross Tonnage

H3E – Single sideband, full carrier

HF – The High Frequency band 3–30MHz used for long-range communication via the ionosphere

IMO – International Maritime Organisation. The United Nations organisation governing maritime affairs and based in London

INMARSAT-A – The original, analogue, satellite communications system. Now obsolescent

INMARSAT-B – A smaller, improved digital version of INMARSAT-A

INMARSAT-C – Text-only satellite communications system by Telex, Fax and e-mail

INMARSAT-E – The EPIRB system using INMARSAT communication satellites

INMARSAT-M – A small version of INMARSAT-B but with reduced facilities

INMARSAT MINI-M – A miniature version of INMARSAT-M but with reduced coverage

International Channels – Marine VHF channels available to all Marine VHF users, but in practice restricted to certain well-defined uses

Iridium – Worldwide mobile phone system using 66 LEO satellites

ITU – The International Telecommunications Union. The International Governing Body for all landline communications and radio transmissions

J3E – Single sideband, no carrier

kHz – Kilohertz, a measure of radio wave frequency in thousands of cycles per second

LEO – Low Earth Orbit of satellites

MCA – Maritime and Coastguard Agency. The British authority for maritime safety and marine radio qualifications

MF – The Medium Frequency band 300kHz–3MHz used for medium range communication and domestic broadcasting

MHz – Megahertz, a measure of radio wave in millions of cycles per second

Modulation – The technique of adding AF to RF so that the AF reaches a high enough frequency for transmission over long distances

MSI – Maritime Safety Information.

Navtex – The text-only system of broadcasting Maritime Safety Information by radio on 518kHz, 490kHz and 4209.5kHz

OTF/OWF – Optimum Traffic/Working Frequency for HF

Phonetex – A technique allowing the dictation of a Telex message for a ship from a telephone ashore

Private Channel – Channel allocated to a particular user and therefore not available for general use

PTT Switch – Press-To-Talk Switch, employed on simplex equipment to switch from receive to transmit mode

Public correspondence channel – Dual-frequency international channel employed for telephone system link-up; designed for duplex operation but also available for simplex-equipped stations

Radio station – Any radio equipped building, ship or aircraft which has been allocated a callsign

R3E – Pilot carrier to ease tuning of the clarifier in SSB receivers

RF – Radio Frequencies – all those between 9kHz and visible light

R/T – Radiotelephone (speech)

SafetyNET – The INMARSAT equivalent of Navtex

SAR – Search And Rescue

SART – Search and Rescue (Radar) Transponder

Selcall – Selective calling system: a transmitted code which alerts a particular radio station. Used only for Telex

Semi-duplex – Used in ship/shore correspondence when the simplex equipment of the vessel makes the simplex procedure essential, despite the shore station having duplex equipment

Ship's Radio Licence – Obligatory for all vessels equipped with marine R/T

Simplex – Single frequency system allowing a radio station to receive or transmit but not both at the same time

SOLAS – Safety of Life at Sea Convention

Squelch – Circuit employed in radio sets to suppress background noise

TOR – Telex Over Radio: allows the transmission of printed text to and from Telex and fax machines

Traffic List – List broadcast by Coast Radio Stations to inform vessels that correspondents wish to make contact via the telephone system

UHF – Ultra High Frequencies of 300MHZ–3GHz. Used by merchant ships for onboard communications and in harbours

VFO – Variable Frequency Oscillator

VHF – Very High Frequency: the frequency range 30–300MHz, part of which is used by short range marine radiotelephones

Working Channel – The channel on which business is transacted following contact on Channel 16 or 2182kHz

W/T – Wireless Telegraphy (Morse)

Important GMDSS

Frequencies

Frequencies indicated in **bold** are particularly vital to remember for the LRC Examination

518 kHz	**International Navtex. (Also 490kHz and 4209.5kHz locally)**
2045kHz	Primary International ship-to-shore Coast Radio Station traffic
2048kHz	Primary international intership traffic & secondary CRS traffic
2177kHz	DSC ship-to-ship calling and acknowledgement
2182kHz	**Voice Distress traffic**
2187.5kHz	**DSC Distress, Urgency, Safety Alerts and Acknowledgement**
2189.5kHz	DSC routine alert to CRS. (Acknowledgement on 2177 kHz)
8414.5kHz	**Main HF DSC Distress Alerts; mandatory watch in Sea Area A3/A4**
121.5MHz	Secondary EPIRB frequency for RDF pin-point location
406MHz	**Primary EPIRB frequency for Distress Alerts and location**
1.6GHz	**Satellite or 'L-Band' EPIRBs**
9GHz	**SART transponders and ship's 3cm radar**
Channel 6	**VHF primary intership and SAR channel - mandatory fit**
Channel 8	VHF secondary intership channel. (Also Channels 72 & 77)
Channel 12	VHF primary channel for port operations and ship movement
Channel 13	**VHF channel for intership safety; watch kept in coastal waters**
Channel 14	VHF secondary channel for port operations and ship movement
Channel 16	**VHF channel for calling, Distress traffic, Urgency and Safety calls**
Channel 67	**VHF primary working channel for HM Coastguard**
Channel 70	**VHF DSC Distress, Urgency, Safety alerts and routine calls**

Useful Frequencies (Not required for LRC exam)

2051kHz	
2054kHz	Additional international ship-to-shore (CRS) frequencies
2057kHz	
2261-2495kHz	Any frequency within these limits in 3kHz increments for intership
3340-3397kHz	communication between vessels of the same nationality
3500-3596kHz	Suggestions: 2300, 2333, 2345, 2444, 2468 kHz, etc.
2635kHz	Additional international intership frequencies in Regions 2 and 3
2638kHz	(see page 77)
4209; 6313kHz	
8416; 12,578kHz	Some HF Ship-to-Ship DSC Individual Alerts
16,806; 18,899kHz	
22,375; 25,209kHz	

USEFUL ADDRESSES

Radio Regulatory Authorities

UK OFCOM (from late 2003)
Riverside House, 2A Southwark
Bridge Road, LONDON SE1 9HA, UK

USA Federal Communications
Commision,
PO Box 1040, PA 17325, USA

CAN Standards Officer,
Authorization Spectrum Mangement,
Operations Directorate,
Department of Communications,
Radio Regulatory Branch,
300, Slater St., OTTAWA, Ontario,
K1A OC8, Canada

❑ There are District or Sub-offices in
most major cities and towns but also
Regional Offices (Moncton, NB;
Montreal, Que.; Toronto, Ont.;
Winnipeg, Man. and Vancouver, BC)

AUS Dept. of Transport & Communication
Radiocommunications Operations
Branch,
GPO Box 594,
CANBERRA, ACT 2601, Australia

❑ (Branches in NSW, Queensland,
South Australia, Tasmania, Victoria,
Western Australia, Australian Capitol
Territory and Northern Territory)

NZ Ministry of Commerce,
Radio Frequency Service,
PO Box 2847,
33, Bowen St., WELLINGTON,
New Zealand

❑ (Field Offices in most major towns)

SA The Senior Manager, Radio and
Terminal Equipment,
Dept. of Posts & Telecommunication,
Private Bag X74, PRETORIA, 0001,
South Africa

EIRE Marine Radio Survey Office,
Room 213, Department of Tourism,
Transport and Communication,
Scotch House,
Hawkins St, DUBLIN, 2,
Republic of Ireland

Amateur Radio Organisations

UK Radio Society of Great Britain,
Lambda House, Cranborne Rd,
POTTERS BAR, Herts., EN6 3JE, UK
(Oversees UK Amateur Radio
Licences)

USA American Radio Relay League,
225, Main Street,
NEWINGTON, Conn. 0611, USA

CAN Canadian Radio Relay League, Inc.
PO Box 7009, Station C, LONDON,
Ontario, N5Y 4J9
Canada

AUS Wireless Institute of Australia,
PO Box 300,
CAULFIELD SOUTH,
Victoria, 3126
Australia

NZ NZART,
  PO Box 40-525,
  UPPER HUTT,
  New Zealand

SA South African Radio Relay League,
  PO Box 3911,
  8000 CAPETOWN,
  South Africa

EIRE Irish Radio Transmitters Society,
  PO Box 462,
  DUBLIN 9,
  Republic of Ireland

GIB Gibraltar Amateur Radio Society,
  PO Box 292,
  GIBRALTAR

Others

Radio Licensing Centre,
  PO Box 885,
  BRISTOL,
  BS99 5LG
UK

(Issues UK Ship, CB and Amateur Radio Licences)

Maritime and Coastguard Agency,
  105 Commercial Road,
  SOUTHAMPTON, SO15 1EG
UK

(Oversees UK Marine Radio Operator Certificates)

AMERC, The Hon. Secretary,:
  check www.amerc.ac.uk for details of their current name and address

(Conducts UK SSB/LRC Marine Radio Operator Exams)

The Royal Yachting Association (RYA),
  RYA House,
  Ensign Way,
  HAMBLE,
  Southampton,
  SO31 4YA
  UK
  (Conducts UK VHF/SRC Manine Radio Operators exams)

You rely on us.
Can we rely on you?

Become an Offshore member from just £4.50 per month.

Last year, our volunteers saved over 7,000 people. But we couldn't have saved a single one of them without the support of people like you. Join Offshore today, and you'll be helping to run the Lifeboat service whose volunteers will be on hand, should you ever get into difficulty at sea.

Call **0800 543210** today.

Or visit **www.lifeboats.org.uk**

Lifeboats
Offshore

FOS2003   registered charity no. 209603